MW00610619

A Cookbook for
WINTER

A Cookbook for
WINTER

MORE THAN 95 NURTURING & COMFORTING RECIPES FOR THE COLDER MONTHS

With recipes by
LOUISE PICKFORD

RYLAND PETERS & SMALL
LONDON • NEW YORK

Senior Designer Toni Kay
Senior Editor Abi Waters
Editorial Director Julia Charles
Production Manager Gordana Simakovic
Creative Director Leslie Harrington
Indexer Vanessa Bird

First published in 2024 by
Ryland Peters & Small
20–21 Jockey's Fields
London WC1R 4BW
and
341 E 116th St
New York NY 10029
www.rylandpeters.com

10 9 8 7 6 5 4 3 2 1

Recipe collection compiled by Julia Charles.
Text copyright © Julia Charles, Carol Hilker,
Kathy Kordalis, Theo A. Michaels, Hannah
Miles, Louise Pickford, Shelagh Ryan, David
T. Smith and Ryland Peters & Small 2024.
Design and photographs copyright
© Ryland Peters & Small 2024
See page 192 for full credits.

Illustration credit Adobe Stock: Nataliiaku:
Cover and pages 3, 8, 46, 82, 134, 148 and 176.

ISBN: 978-1-78879-646-0

The authors' moral rights have been
asserted. All rights reserved. No part of this
publication may be reproduced, stored in a
retrieval system, or transmitted in any form
or by any means, electronic, mechanical,
photocopying, or otherwise, without the
prior permission of the publisher.

A CIP record for this book is available
rom the British Library.

US Library of Congress cataloging-in-
publication data has been applied for.

Printed and bound in China

NOTES

• Both American (Imperial plus US cups)
and British (Metric) measurements and
ingredients are included in these recipes for
your convenience, however it is important to
work with one set of measurements and not
alternate between the two within a recipe.
• All spoon measurements are level unless
otherwise specified.
• Many recipes in this book call for a Dutch
oven. This is a thick-walled cooking pot with
a tight-fitting lid. Any cast iron or ceramic
casserole dish can be used – they are ideal for
sautéing, braising, slow-cooking and baking
so come into their own in the winter months.
If a recipe is cooked only on the hob/stovetop
a large saucepan can usually be substituted.
• When a recipe calls for the zest of citrus
fruit, buy unwaxed fruit and wash well before
using. If you can only find treated fruit, scrub
well in warm soapy water before using.
• Ovens should be preheated to the specified
temperatures. We recommend using an oven
thermometer. If using a fan-assisted oven,
adjust temperatures according to the
manufacturer's instructions.

FSC
www.fsc.org

MIX
Paper from
responsible sources
FSC® C106563

Contents

Introduction

In A Cookbook for Winter, *every recipe is an invitation to gather around the table for shared moments of joy and warmth.*

As the mercury dips, our culinary inclinations lean towards comfort foods – those warming recipes that are akin to a hug for the soul during the cold days. Winter cooking is characterized by hearty stews and rich soups that simmer on the stovetop and slow-cooked casseroles and savoury pies that bubble in the oven, filling homes with enticing aromas. These dishes often feature seasonal produce, which not only provide depth of flavour but also essential nutrients to bolster our health through the colder months, encouraging adventures in both taste and nourishment.

In the heart of winter, when the air is crisp and the landscape is blanketed in snow, our kitchens can become havens of warmth and creativity. This season beckons us to explore a rich tapestry of ingredients that thrive in the chill. Pumpkin and squashes with their hardy shells, reveal vibrant, nutrient-dense flesh. Hardy greens such as kale and chard withstand frosty temperatures and offer a welcome burst of colour to many dishes, as does radicchio when it makes its debut in December. Incorporating grains and pulses/ legumes adds both texture and sustenance, and the comfort of melting cheese, spiked with a little warming spirit in a fondue cannot be underestimated; it is no coincidence that this is food born of snow-capped mountains. Citrus fruits also peak during these months, orange zest and juice adding brightness to counterbalance

the hearty fare, along with the heady sweetness of ripe pears. Spices play a pivotal role too: cinnamon, nutmeg, cloves and ginger enhance flavour and bring with them their own comforting warmth. These star ingredients not only inspire culinary exploration but also connect us to nature's rhythm, making cooking at this time of year uniquely satisfying.

Embracing winter cooking is also perhaps about more than just adjusting our diets to the colder weather. It's a time when meals become more than just sustenance; they turn into moments of connection and warmth shared with loved ones around the table. As the frost blankets the world in its serene white, the pleasure of eating together becomes a cherished ritual. In these chilly times, kitchens and dining rooms transform into warm havens full of comforting scents; it's a celebration of the season's unique offerings and an opportunity to create warmth and contentment in our homes. This time of year, we are encouraged to slow down, take the time to savour each meal, and explore recipes that embody the essence of winter.

Whether it is perfecting a traditional recipe or experimenting with seasonal produce, winter cooking is an art that nourishes both body and spirit and we hope you find all the inspiration and encouragement you need in the recipes that follow.

Snow day soups & snacks

Slowly braised onions are truly one of life's pleasures, especially in this classic, comforting soup, with its topping of melted cheese. For vegetarians, if you are happy eating cheese, simply replace the beef or chicken stock with vegetable stock.

Baked French onion soup with Gruyère topping

75 ml/5 tablespoons extra virgin olive oil

1 kg/2 lb. 4 oz. onions, thinly sliced

2 garlic cloves, finely chopped

2 teaspoons freshly chopped thyme

125 ml/½ cup fruity red wine

1 litre/4 cups beef stock or chicken stock (see page 19)

½ French baguette

75 g/⅔ cup grated Gruyère

2 tablespoons grated Parmesan

sea salt and freshly ground black pepper

Serves 4

Preheat the oven to 180°C fan/200°C/400°F/Gas 6.

Heat the oil in a 4-litre/quart Dutch oven over a medium heat and gently fry the onions, garlic and thyme with a little salt and pepper for 25 minutes until really soft and lightly golden, stirring frequently to prevent the onions from burning.

Add the wine, bring to the boil and boil for 5 minutes or until evaporated, then pour in the stock. Bring back to the boil and season to taste.

Cut the bread into slices 1 cm/½ inch thick and arrange over the top of the soup. Scatter over the Gruyère and Parmesan cheeses and transfer the pan to the preheated oven. Bake uncovered for about 10–15 minutes until the soup is bubbling and the cheese melted and golden. If you wish, you can brown the top of the cheese under a hot broiler/grill.

Cool for 10 minutes before serving.

Pangrattato is an Italian fried breadcrumb garnish, often scattered over a dish of cooked pasta. Here, combined with crispy fried bacon, it provides both crunch and flavour to the finished bean soup.

White bean & rosemary soup with bacon pangrattato

60 ml/4 tablespoons olive oil, plus extra to serve

1 large onion, chopped

2 garlic cloves, crushed

2 tablespoons freshly chopped rosemary

350 g/12 oz. potatoes, such as Yukon Gold, Russet, Desiree, or King Edward, diced into 1-cm/½-inch cubes

2 x 400-g/14-oz. cans cannellini or haricot beans, drained and rinsed (see introduction)

1 litre/4 cups chicken stock or vegetable stock

2 bay leaves

sea salt and freshly ground black pepper

BACON PANGRATTATO

60 ml/4 tablespoons olive oil

125 g/4½ oz. rashers/slices of bacon, rind removed and diced

1 large garlic clove, crushed

100 g/3½ oz. day-old bread (without crusts)

2 tablespoons freshly chopped flat-leaf parsley

Serves 4–6

Heat the oil in a 4-litre/quart Dutch oven over a medium heat and fry the onion, garlic and rosemary for 5 minutes until lightly golden. Add the potatoes and beans, stir well and then add the stock, bay leaves and a little salt and pepper. Bring to the boil, then lower the heat and simmer gently for 15–20 minutes until the potatoes are tender.

Meanwhile, make the pangrattato. Heat the oil in a medium frying pan/skillet over a high heat. Add the bacon and fry for 2–3 minutes until crisp and golden. Remove the pan from the heat and using a slotted spoon, remove the bacon from the oil, and set aside. Add the garlic to the hot oil off the heat and set aside for 10 minutes to flavour it. Remove and discard the garlic.

Cut the bread into pieces and place in a food processor. Using the pulse button, blend the bread to make rough crumbs, as evenly sized as you can. Return the frying pan/skillet to a medium-high heat, add the breadcrumbs and cook, stirring, for 5 minutes or until they are evenly golden and crisp. Combine with the bacon, parsley and a little salt and pepper and set aside.

When the potatoes are tender, transfer half the soup to a blender or food processor (or use a stick blender) and blend until smooth. Return to the pan and stir. Taste and adjust the seasoning, then heat through.

Divide the soup between warm bowls and top with the pangrattato and a swirl of olive oil.

Pumpkin soup is a classic to serve at Halloween or for Bonfire Night – it freezes well so you can prepare ahead and then just defrost and reheat on the day. For an extra spooky treat, why not serve in roasted pumpkin bowls – once the soup is eaten you can eat the bowl too. Small pumpkins and squashes work perfectly for this (see tip below).

Roasted pumpkin soup

1.3 kg/3 lb. pumpkin or butternut squash, peeled and roughly chopped

grated zest and freshly squeezed juice of 1 orange

1 teaspoon ground ginger

3 tablespoons olive oil

1 litre/4 cups chicken or vegetable stock

sea salt and freshly ground black pepper

double/heavy cream, to serve

toasted mixed seeds, to serve

Serves 4

Preheat the oven to 160°C fan/180°C/350°F/Gas 4.

Place the chopped squash or pumpkin in a roasting pan and sprinkle over the orange zest and juice, ginger and olive oil. Roast in the preheated oven for 20–30 minutes until the squash is soft when you cut it with a knife.

Remove from the oven and place in a saucepan with the stock over a medium heat. Bring to the boil, then reduce the heat and simmer for about 15 minutes. Using a stick blender, blender or food processor, blitz until the soup is smooth.

Pour the soup into four bowls and add a swirl of cream to each. Serve topped with toasted seeds.

Tip: If you are making the pumpkin shell bowls, scoop out the insides of four small pumpkins or the round end of four small butternut squashes so that there is a thin layer of flesh remaining on the skin. Use the flesh in the soup recipe above. Drizzle the shells with olive oil and season with salt and pepper and roast in the oven for 25–30 minutes until the flesh is soft but the pumpkin or squash bowl still holds its shape. Serve the soup in the roasted bowls.

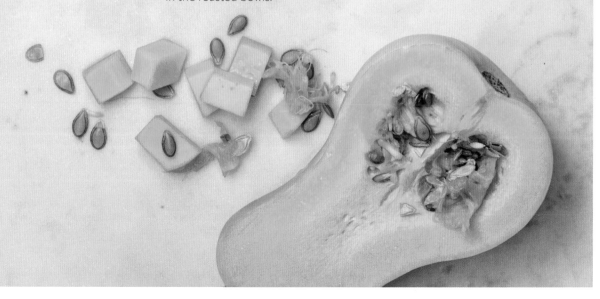

Cauliflower may seem a humble vegetable but in this recipe, it is transformed into a deliciously creamy soup. If you don't have cauliflower, you can substitute broccoli, which works equally well. Also try Cheddar instead of the blue cheese if preferred.

Creamy cauliflower & blue cheese soup

15 g/1 tablespoon butter

1 onion, finely chopped

1 whole cauliflower about 850 g/1 lb. 14 oz., leaves and stalk removed, chopped into pieces

1 litre/4 cups vegetable stock

125 ml/½ cup milk

75 g/2¾ oz. soft blue cheese, crumbled, plus extra to serve (optional)

sea salt and freshly ground black pepper

Serves 4

In a saucepan, melt the butter and fry the onion until soft and translucent. Add the cauliflower to the saucepan together with the stock and simmer until the cauliflower is very soft.

Add the milk to the saucepan and season well with salt and pepper. Add the blue cheese and stir over the heat until it has melted.

Using a stick blender, blender or food processor, blend until smooth and creamy. Season with salt and pepper to taste.

Pour into four bowls and top each with a sprinkling of black pepper and a little extra crumbled blue cheese, if liked.

When cauliflower is roasted it takes on a whole new dimension with a caramelized taste. Almonds add a nutty texture and the puréed cauliflower gives it a creamy feel even though there is no cream or milk added. This recipe is served with cauliflower pickles, which have a sharpness to cut through the creamy texture of the soup. The pickles should be prepared the day before so that they have time to absorb the wonderful vibrant yellow of the saffron.

Roasted cauliflower soup
with toasted almonds & pickled florets

1 head of cauliflower, about
   1 kg/2 lb. 4 oz.

olive oil, to drizzle

1 teaspoon sweet paprika

100 g/¾ cup blanched whole almonds
   (such as marcona)

1 litre/4 cups vegetable or chicken
   stock

4–6 tablespoons crème fraîche
   (optional)

sea salt and freshly ground
   black pepper

PICKLED FLORETS

cauliflower leaves and 1 floret
   (from the main cauliflower)

a pinch of saffron

2 tablespoons cider vinegar

1 tablespoon caster/granulated sugar

Serves 4–6

Begin by making the pickled florets as these are best made the day before. Remove all the leaves from the cauliflower and remove one large floret from the base. Keep the rest of the cauliflower for making the soup. Slice the floret very finely and place in a bowl. Put the saffron into another small bowl, pour a little boiling water over and leave for 5 minutes to steep, then pour into the bowl with the cauliflower slices. Mix the sugar and vinegar together until the sugar has dissolved, and then add to the cauliflower and saffron water. Cover and place in the fridge to soak overnight.

The next day, preheat the oven to 180°C fan/200°C/400°F/Gas 6.

Using a sharp knife, remove the stalk of the cauliflower, but cut carefully to ensure that the head of the cauliflower stays in one piece. Place in the roasting pan, drizzle with a good glug of olive oil and sprinkle with salt, pepper and the paprika. Seal the pan with a layer of aluminium foil. Roast in the preheated oven for 45 minutes, then remove the foil and roast for a further 30–45 minutes until the cauliflower is soft.

About 5 minutes before the end of cooking, add the almonds to the roasting pan and roast for 5 minutes, which should colour the nuts a golden brown. Take care that they do not burn. Remove a handful of the nuts for the garnish and roughly chop them.

Place the cauliflower head (which will by now be really soft) in a large saucepan with the remaining nuts and add the stock. Bring to the boil over a medium heat, then reduce the heat and simmer for 10 minutes. Using a stick blender, blender or food processor, blend until smooth.

Pour into bowls and add a spoonful of crème fraîche, if using, to each portion. Sprinkle with the reserved chopped nuts and the pickled florets.

Curried parsnip soup is one of the most traditional flavours of soup and is always popular. The sweetness of the vegetable pairs perfectly with the spices. This soup is topped with a traditional tadka of ghee with fried spices and curry leaves. I like quite a mild flavour so I use korma curry powder, but you can use a spicier version if you prefer. You can even add a finely sliced red chilli/chile at the same time as the garlic for extra fire. Parsnip crisps also make a fun topping – you can either buy these or follow the instructions in the tip below.

Curried parsnip soup

2 tablespoons ghee

1 onion, chopped

2 garlic cloves, finely chopped

2.5-cm/1-inch piece of ginger, peeled and finely sliced

500 g/1 lb. 2 oz. parsnips, peeled and chopped

1 tablespoon curry powder

1 litre/4 cups vegetable stock

sea salt and freshly ground black pepper

TADKA

2 tablespoons ghee

1 teaspoon cumin seeds

1 teaspoon nigella seeds

12 curry leaves

Serves 4

Heat the ghee in a large saucepan and fry the onion over a gentle heat until soft and translucent. Add the garlic and ginger and fry for few minutes. Add the parsnips and curry powder and cook for a few minutes, then add the stock and simmer until the parsnips are soft.

Using a stick blender, blender or food processor, blitz the soup until smooth, and then season with salt and pepper to taste.

Heat the ghee for the tadka and add the cumin seeds, nigella seeds and curry leaves. Heat for a few minutes until you can smell the spices and the seeds start to pop.

Pour the soup into four bowls and top each with a little of the hot tadka.

Tip: Parsnip crisps make a perfect topping for this soup. Using a swivel peeler or mandoline, cut very thin slices from a parsnip. Toss lightly in a drizzle of olive oil and season well with salt and pepper. Place the strips (stretching them out so that they are flat) on a baking sheet and bake in an oven preheated to 160°C fan/180°C/350°F/Gas 4 for 5–10 minutes until crisp, checking regularly as they can burn quickly.

There isn't a heartier farmhouse soup than pearl barley broth. The barley makes this a really filling soup, but if you don't have any, you can substitute with soup pasta instead. This version is made with lamb, but you can easily substitute with beef and beef stock, if you prefer.

Pearl barley broth

100 g/generous ½ cup pearl barley

1 tablespoon olive oil

1 onion, finely chopped

2 lamb leg steaks
  (about 300 g/10½ oz.)

3 carrots, peeled and cut into
  small cubes

100 ml/⅓ cup plus 1 tablespoon
  white wine

1 litre/4 cups lamb stock

1 heaped teaspoon wholegrain
  mustard

100 g/½ cup frozen peas

sea salt and freshly ground
  black pepper

chopped fresh parsley, to garnish
  (optional)

Serves 4

Rinse the pearl barley. Drain and set aside.

Add the oil and onion to a large saucepan and sauté for about 5 minutes over a medium heat until the onion softens and starts to caramelize.

Cut the lamb steaks into small pieces, trimming away any fat, and add to the saucepan to brown. Once the lamb has browned on all sides, add the carrot pieces to the saucepan and sauté for a few minutes.

Pour in the wine and bring to a simmer, then pour in the lamb stock and 500 ml/2 cups water. Gently simmer the soup for 30 minutes until the pearl barley is soft.

Using a stick blender, blender or food processor, blend a few ladlefuls of the broth (including some barley and carrots), then return it to the soup to thicken it. Add the mustard and season with salt and pepper to taste.

When you are ready to serve, heat the soup, add in the frozen peas and cook for about 5 minutes. Pour into four bowls and serve sprinkled with freshly chopped parsley.

Beans are a great source of protein, especially for anyone on a vegan or vegetarian diet. You can use any beans of your choice for this soup. Canned beans are easy to use because they are already cooked, but you can prepare your own beans, if you prefer, by soaking them overnight and then cooking according to the packet instructions. The chilli/chili sauce with the kidney beans is generally very mild, so if you prefer a spicier heat, add a little chilli/chili powder or some dried chilli flakes/hot red pepper flakes when you add the beans for a fiery kick.

Three bean soup

1 tablespoon olive oil

1 onion, chopped

1 garlic clove, finely chopped

1 yellow (bell) pepper, deseeded and cut into small pieces

1 carrot, peeled and cut into small pieces

1 courgette/zucchini, cut into small pieces

400-g/14-oz. can black beans in water, drained

400-g/14-oz. can cannellini beans in water, drained

400-g/14-oz. can red kidney beans in chilli/chili sauce

400-g/14-oz. can chopped tomatoes

1 tablespoon tomato purée/paste

250 ml/1 cup red wine

1 litre/4 cups chicken or vegetable stock

1 teaspoon dried oregano

a handful of chopped fresh basil, plus extra to serve

100 g/3½ oz. soup pasta

sea salt and freshly ground black pepper

freshly grated Parmesan or Cheddar, to serve

Serves 6

In a large saucepan, heat the olive oil and fry the onion until soft and translucent. Add the chopped garlic and fry until lightly golden brown, then add the chopped yellow pepper, carrot and courgette and fry for a few minutes to soften.

Rinse the drained black beans and cannellini beans well in cold water. Add them to the saucepan along with the kidney beans in chilli sauce, chopped tomatoes, tomato purée, red wine, stock, oregano and basil and simmer for 30 minutes.

Add the soup pasta to the saucepan and simmer for the time stated on the pasta instructions – usually about 8–10 minutes – until the pasta is cooked. Season well with salt and pepper.

Using a stick blender, blender or food processor, blitz the soup quickly – you want to leave most of the soup in chunks, but blending some of the mixture will help thicken the soup. Taste for seasoning adding more salt and pepper as needed.

Divide the soup between six bowls and serve with freshly grated Parmesan or Cheddar and some extra chopped basil leaves.

This hearty soup is the perfect nourishment after a long snowy trek through the woods, drinking schnapps, followed by steaming bowls of cabbage and sausage. It has a meaty broth with sweetness from the cider and a tang of mustard seeds. If you prefer not to make the sausage balls, you can use cooked whole sausages instead and just cut them into slices and add to the soup. Make sure they are heated through in the soup broth before serving. To avoid having to slurp too much with this soup, make sure you cut the cabbage into short, finely shredded pieces.

Sausage & cabbage soup

3 pork sausages

1 tablespoon olive oil

1 large onion, finely chopped

125 g/4½ oz. bacon lardons

1 garlic clove, finely chopped

a large sprig of fresh rosemary

1 heaped teaspoon wholegrain mustard

300 ml/1¼ cups pear or apple cider

700 ml/scant 3 cups beef stock

1 small Savoy cabbage, stalk and outer leaves removed, finely shredded and rinsed

sea salt and freshly ground black pepper

roasting pan, lined with baking parchment

Serves 4

Preheat the oven to 160°C fan/180°C/350°F/Gas 4.

Remove the skins from the sausages and roll the meat into small balls, about 6 or 7 from each sausage. You need them to be small enough to eat in a mouthful of soup. Place them in the lined roasting pan and bake in the oven for about 10 minutes until they are lightly golden brown, turning regularly so that they are golden brown all over. Drain on paper towels to remove any excess fat. Set aside while you prepare the soup.

In a large saucepan, heat the oil over a medium heat and fry the onions until soft and translucent. Add the lardons, garlic and rosemary to the saucepan and fry for a few minutes until the bacon is cooked through. Add the mustard to the saucepan and fry for 1 minute, then add the cider and stock, bring to a simmer and cook over a low heat for 15 minutes.

Add the finely shredded cabbage to the saucepan and continue to simmer for about 10 minutes until the cabbage is soft. Add the reserved sausage balls to the pan and heat for a further 5 minutes.

Season with salt and pepper, tasting before adding too much salt as the soup will already contain some salt from the bacon. Remove the rosemary sprig before serving into bowls, making sure that the sausage balls are evenly distributed.

There are few things more comforting than a baked potato – and this soup takes all the flavours of a jacket with the addition of caramelized butter for a bit of luxury. Rich and creamy with sour cream and grated cheese, this is a perfect soup for cold winter days.

Brown butter baked potato soup

4 large baking potatoes

110 g/1 stick butter

1 litre/4 cups chicken or
vegetable stock

150 ml/²⁄₃ cup sour cream

100 g/1 cup plus 2 tablespoons
grated Cheddar

olive oil, to drizzle

sea salt and freshly ground
black pepper

POTATO SKINS

potato skins, reserved from
the baked potatoes

olive oil, to drizzle

30 g/¹⁄₃ cup grated Cheddar

Serves 4

Preheat the oven to 180°C fan/200°C/400°F/Gas 6.

Prick the potatoes with a fork, rub the skins with a little salt and bake in the preheated oven for about 1 hour until the potatoes are soft when you insert a sharp knife into the centre. Set aside until cool enough to handle without burning yourself.

In a saucepan, melt the butter over a gentle heat until it starts to lightly brown – the butter will smell nutty which is how you will know it is ready. Scoop out the potato from the skins (reserving the skins for the garnish) and add to the butter. Cook for a few minutes, then add the stock and simmer for 5–10 minutes. Add the sour cream and grated cheese, then blitz the soup in a blender or food processor until smooth, or use a stick blender. Pour the soup back into the saucepan, season with salt and pepper to taste and keep warm.

For the potato skins, preheat the grill/broiler to high. Place the reserved skins on a baking sheet and drizzle with a little olive oil. Sprinkle with the grated cheese and season with salt and pepper. Place under the hot grill and grill/broil until the cheese has melted and the skins are crispy – this will take about 5 minutes, but watch them carefully as grills are all different and you don't want them to burn.

Serve the soup in bowls with a drizzle of olive oil and the crispy potato skins broken up on top or served whole on the side.

As everyone knows, garlic can have quite a pungent taste, but when it is roasted it softens and caramelizes and takes on the wonderfully earthy notes of forest walks and mushrooms. If you want, you can add mushrooms as well to give the soup more body. Don't be scared about using four whole bulbs of garlic here!

Roasted garlic soup

30 g/2 tablespoons butter

2 large onions, finely chopped

60 ml/¼ cup brandy

1 litre/4 cups beef stock

freshly squeezed juice of ½ lemon

ROASTED GARLIC

a large sprig of fresh rosemary

a few sprigs of fresh thyme

strips of zest from 1 lemon

4 whole garlic bulbs

olive oil, to drizzle

sea salt and freshly ground black pepper

Serves 4

Preheat the oven to 160°C fan/180°C/350°F/Gas 4.

Start by making the roasted garlic. Place the rosemary, thyme and lemon zest strips in a roasting pan and put the four whole garlic bulbs on top of the herbs. Drizzle the bulbs with a good drizzle of olive oil and season with salt and pepper. Roast in the preheated oven for 25–30 minutes until the bulbs feel soft inside when you press them. Leave to cool.

Once the garlic bulbs are cool, cut them in half with a sharp knife and squeeze out the garlic, which will be creamy and paste like. Discard all of the garlic skins, making sure that no skin is left in the garlic paste. Reserve some of the roasted thyme to garnish the soup and discard the other herbs and the zest.

For the soup, heat the butter in a saucepan over a medium heat and fry the onions in the butter until soft and translucent and starting to caramelize. Add the garlic purée and cook for a few minutes more. Add the brandy and cook until it is almost evaporated, then add the stock and lemon juice, bring it to a simmer and then cook over a low heat for about 10 minutes.

Using a stick blender, blender or food processor, blitz the soup until smooth, or use a stick blender. Taste and adjust the seasoning, and then serve i n bowls with the reserved sprigs of roasted thyme to garnish.

Tip: If you prefer a thicker texture soup you can add 2 peeled and cubed potatoes with the stock and simmer until the potatoes are soft.

Classic, moreish, crowd-pleasing and just simply delicious. This is the perfect way to use up leftover risotto, or just make them from scratch. You can stuff the arancini with an array of fillings, from mozzarella to goat's cheese or chopped ham. This recipe uses pecorino – a hard sheep's milk cheese, with a tangy taste – while the addition of ricotta adds a creaminess.

Pecorino arancini with roasted cherry tomato sauce

50 ml/3½ tablespoons olive oil

1 onion, finely chopped

2 garlic cloves, crushed

200 g/generous 1 cup Arborio risotto rice

750 ml/3 cups vegetable stock

5 sprigs lemon thyme, leaves picked

150 g/5½ oz. pecorino (²/₃ grated and ¹/₃ cut into 20 cubes)

100 g/scant ½ cup ricotta

½ teaspoon ground nutmeg

plain/all-purpose flour, for coating

2 eggs, lightly beaten

250 g/4½ cups fine soft white breadcrumbs

sunflower oil, for deep-frying

ROASTED CHERRY TOMATO SAUCE

500 g/1 lb. 2 oz. cherry tomatoes on the vine

4 garlic cloves, smashed

3 tablespoons olive oil

2 tablespoons honey

a pinch of dried chilli flakes/hot red pepper flakes

sea salt and freshly ground black pepper

20 g/²/₃ oz. fresh lemon thyme, leaves picked, to garnish

Serves 4–6

Heat the oil in a saucepan over a low heat, add the onion and stir occasionally until tender. Add the crushed garlic and the rice, stir to coat, then add the stock, little by little, until the rice is slightly overcooked and the stock is absorbed. Add the thyme, grated pecorino, ricotta and nutmeg and stir until creamy. Remove from heat and spread the mixture out in a tray. Cool to room temperature, then refrigerate for 1–1½ hours.

Meanwhile, make the sauce. Preheat the oven to 160°C fan/180°C/350°F/Gas 4. In a baking dish, add the tomatoes on the vine with the garlic cloves, 2 tablespoons of the olive oil, the honey, dried chilli flakes and salt and pepper. Roast in the preheated oven for 25 minutes, then add a few tablespoons of water, remove the vine and crush the tomatoes. Set aside.

Shape walnut-sized balls of the chilled rice mixture with your hands, then push a pecorino cube into centre of each, pressing rice around to enclose completely. Roll the rice balls in flour, then in beaten egg and finally in breadcrumbs, shaking off excess in between, ensuring they are completely coated. Place on a tray and chill in the fridge for 30 minutes.

Preheat the oil in a deep saucepan or deep-fryer to 200°C/400°F. Deep-fry the arancini in batches for 2–3 minutes until golden brown and crispy, turning occasionally.

Place the roasted cherry tomato sauce on serving plates, drizzle over the remaining olive oil and serve with the hot crispy arancini to top, scattered with thyme leaves.

Bagna cauda is a rich garlic and anchovy dip from Piedmont in the north of Italy. It isn't strictly a fondue, but is traditionally served hot from a small fondue dish. Serve with a selection of vegetables, including chicory/endive leaves, fennel, celery and cardoons (a relative of the artichoke). Other choices are sweet peppers, mushrooms, carrots, cherry tomatoes, cauliflower and regular artichoke hearts. It's also marvellous just with bread or grissini for dipping.

Bagna cauda

200 ml/³⁄₄ cup extra virgin olive oil

4–5 garlic cloves, crushed

12 anchovy fillets, mashed, about 50–75 g/2–2½ oz.

60 g/4 tablespoons walnut paste or almond butter, or 2 tablespoons each of walnut oil and butter

TO SERVE

a selection of vegetables, trimmed and cut into bite-sized pieces

crusty bread or breadsticks (optional)

metal fondue pot and tabletop burner

Serves 4–6 as an appetizer

Put the oil, garlic and anchovies into a small saucepan and heat gently on the stovetop, taking care not to brown the garlic. Stir in the walnut paste or walnut oil and butter and cook for 2–3 minutes.

Transfer to a fondue pot and set over a tabletop burner to keep the mixture warm. Serve with the vegetables and bread, if using, for dipping.

Variation: *Creamy Bagna Cauda*
Put 400 ml/1²⁄₃ cups single/light cream into a small saucepan and bring to the boil. Simmer until reduced by half – about 5 minutes. Put 1 tablespoon butter into a small fondue pot and melt over a low heat. Add 12 anchovy fillets, finely chopped, and 4 crushed garlic cloves and cook briefly, mashing together and taking care not to let the garlic brown. Stir in the reduced cream and transfer the bowl to its tabletop burner to keep warm. Serve with vegetables and bread.

This intriguing deep-fried, dome-shaped mound of cheese on a round of bread is a fancier version of a malakoff from Switzerland. It most likely would have been enjoyed by farmers tending their sheep, frying bits of cheese to sustain them during the cold months. It is best served with a glass of chilled dry but fruity white wine as an appetizer.

Swiss fondue fritters

8 slices white bread, such as
  a country loaf

250 g/9 oz. Gruyère, Emmental
  or Tomme, grated as finely
  as possible

1½ tablespoons plain/all-purpose flour

1 teaspoon Dijon mustard

1 egg, beaten

a pinch of cayenne pepper

2 tablespoons dry white wine

sea salt and freshly ground black
  pepper

sunflower oil, for frying

sweet chilli sauce, to serve

a 6-cm/2½-inch cookie cutter

Serves 4

Using the cookie cutter, stamp out a round from each slice of bread.

Combine the grated cheese, flour, mustard, egg, cayenne and salt and pepper in a bowl and work together. Then stir in the wine to form a coarse paste.

Carefully place a spoonful of the paste on top of each circle of bread and using wet hands, shape the mound into a smooth dome about 3 cm/1¼ inch in height.

Pour oil to a depth of roughly 5 cm/2 inches into a heavy-based pan or fondue pot and heat to 180°C/350°F or until a cube of bread crisps in 30 seconds. Very gently lower the fritters, two at a time and cheese side down, into the hot oil and fry for about 3 minutes. Then flip them over and fry for a further 1 minute until they are golden brown (the bread base will always be darker than the domed top). Keep warm in the oven while cooking the rest.

Serve the fritters immediately with some sweet chilli sauce.

This is the perfect in-front-of-the-fire sharing snack. You make a ring of pizza dough and pop a whole Camembert in the centre, bake until the bread is risen and golden and the cheese melted and utterly delicious. Serve with bread or roasted veggies to dip, plus a glass of beer!

Pizza ring with melted camembert

2 teaspoons dried active yeast

140–150 ml/9–10 tablespoons warmed water

1 tablespoon caster/granulated sugar

250 g/1¾ cups white bread flour, plus extra for dusting

2 teaspoons freshly chopped rosemary, plus extra for cooking

1 teaspoon sea salt

1 tablespoon extra virgin olive oil, plus extra for oiling and drizzling

1 whole Camembert

freshly ground black pepper

roasted vine-ripened cherry tomatoes, to serve

25-cm/10-inch cake pan or pizza tray

Serves 4–6

Place the yeast in a bowl, add 50 ml/3½ tablespoons of the water, the sugar and 1 tablespoon of the flour and stir well. Let sit for 10 minutes until the mixture is frothy.

Combine the remaining flour, rosemary and salt in a bowl and work in the frothy yeast mixture, olive oil and enough of the remaining water to bring the mixture together to form a soft dough. Transfer to a lightly floured surface and knead for 5–8 minutes until smooth and elastic. Shape the dough into a ball and place in a lightly oiled bowl, cover with cling film/plastic wrap and leave to rise for 1 hour or until doubled in size.

Tip the dough out onto a lightly floured surface and knock out the air. Roll the dough up into a log about 25 cm/ 10 inches in length and cut into 16 equal slices. Place them in a ring around the sides of the cake pan or pizza tray. Cover with oiled cling film/plastic wrap and leave to rise for 1 hour.

Preheat the oven to 180°C fan/200°C/400°F/Gas 6.

Remove the Camembert from its box and place it in the centre of the dough ring. Score the Camembert in a diamond pattern and drizzle with oil, adding some rosemary sprigs and salt and pepper. Transfer to the preheated oven and bake for about 20 minutes until the bread is risen and golden and the cheese melted. Cool for 5–10 minutes before serving with some roasted cherry tomatoes.

These little polenta/cornmeal cubes, crispy on the outside, soft and creamy on the inside make a great appetizer served with the tangy herb dip. The polenta is best made ahead of time so it can set firmly before being cubed and dipped into extra polenta crumbs. Serve with a glass of crisp, dry white wine.

Polenta fries with mayonnaise & chimichurri

1½ teaspoons sea salt

75 g/½ cup instant polenta/
cornmeal, plus 4 tablespoons
extra for crumb coating

30 g/2 tablespoons butter

30 g/½ cup freshly grated Parmesan

freshly ground black pepper

sunflower oil, for deep-frying

mayonnaise, to serve

CHIMICHURRI SAUCE

15 g/½ oz. fresh coriander/cilantro

15 g/½ oz. fresh parsley

1 teaspoon dried oregano

2 garlic cloves, chopped

½ teaspoon smoked paprika

150 ml/⅔ cup extra virgin olive oil

1 tablespoon red wine vinegar

a pinch of caster/granulated sugar

*20-cm/8-inch square baking pan
lined with baking paper*

metal fondue pan and tabletop burner

Serves 6–8

Bring 500 ml/2 cups water to the boil in a heavy-based saucepan, add the salt and then stir in the polenta/cornmeal. Cook over a medium heat, stirring with a wooden spoon for 4–5 minutes or until the polenta is paste-like and comes away from the sides of the pan.

Remove from the heat and immediately stir in the butter, Parmesan and some black pepper. Pour the paste into the prepared pan, spread flat and set aside until completely cold. Turn the polenta out onto a board and cut into 2-cm/¾-inch cubes. Put the 4 tablespoons of polenta in a shallow bowl, add the cubes and turn to coat well. Arrange on a larger platter.

To make the chimichurri sauce, place all the ingredients in a food processor or blender and blend until fairly smooth. Season to taste and spoon into a bowl. Place on the table along with the platter of polenta cubes and bowls of mayonnaise.

Heat enough oil to come no more than a third of the way up the sides of a metal fondue pan and heat on the stovetop until it reaches 180°C/350°F. As soon as the oil reaches temperature, very carefully transfer the pot to the tabletop burner. Diners can now skewer the polenta cubes and cook, in batches, in the hot oil for about 2–3 minutes until golden and heated through. Serve with the chimichurri and mayonnaise.

Sweet and savoury combine here as an appetizer, rather than a dessert, as the sharpness of the cheese is just enough for the honey to sweeten slightly but not overpower, therefore providing the perfect balance in a super simple dish.

Goat's cheese rounds with honey, thyme & grapes

6 slices smoked bacon (optional)

200 g/7 oz. goat's cheese log

1–2 tablespoons clear honey

2 teaspoons picked thyme leaves

1 teaspoon fennel seeds, roughly ground

1 tablespoon sesame seeds

1 tablespoon walnut oil

freshly ground black pepper

grapes, ripe pears and walnut bread, to serve

raclette (optional)

Serves 6

Dry fry the bacon slices, if using, in a frying pan/skillet over a high heat until crisped to your liking.

Heat the raclette machine or a conventional grill/broiler to the highest setting. Cut the cheese log into 6 x 1-cm/½ -inch slices and place each slice on a raclette tray. Top each with a little honey, thyme, ground fennel and sesame seeds. Season with pepper and drizzle with a little walnut oil.

Place the goat's cheese under the grill/broiler and cook for 5–6 minutes until it is melted and bubbling. At the same time, reheat the bacon slices on the hot plate of the raclette machine (or in the frying pan/skillet) for 2–3 minutes.

Scrape the cooked cheese onto plates and serve with the bacon, slices of walnut bread, some sweet grapes and nicely ripe pears.

Nothing to do with rabbits, of course (you may know this dish as Welsh rarebit)! Many countries have a version of the perennially popular cheese melted on toast – French croque monsieur, Italian mozzarella in carozza, while this Welsh classic is a particularly creamy version.

Welsh rabbit with mustard onions

225 g/8 oz. Cheddar, grated

15 g/1 tablespoon softened butter

2 teaspoons Worcestershire sauce

1 teaspoon mustard powder

2 teaspoons plain/all-purpose flour

a pinch of cayenne pepper

60 ml/¼ cup light beer

MUSTARD ONIONS

250 ml/1 cup verjuice or
  white rice vinegar (see note)

4 tablespoons sugar

1 tablespoon wholegrain mustard

300 g/10½ oz. silverskin/cocktail
  onions, rinsed thoroughly

TO SERVE

4 English muffins or thick slices
  of bread, toasted

grilled/broiled slices of bacon
  (optional)

blanched asparagus (optional)

Serves 4

First make the mustard onions. Put the verjuice or vinegar and sugar into a small non-reactive saucepan and heat until dissolved. Bring to the boil and reduce by half, about 5 minutes. Remove from the heat and stir in the mustard and onions. Let marinate for at least 1 hour.

Place the cheese in a saucepan with the remaining ingredients and stir well. Place over a low heat and stir until the mixture is just melted and forms a paste. Remove from the heat and cool for 2–3 minutes.

Put the toasted muffins onto 4 serving plates and pour over the melted cheese mixture. The rabbits may be grilled/broiled to brown the cheese, or left plain. Top with bacon and asparagus, if using. Serve with the mustard onions on the side.

Note: Verjuice – an acidic juice made from unripe grapes – is available in some delicatessens. If unavailable, use white rice vinegar instead.

Fondues &
fireside suppers

Neuchâtel is a lakeside city in Switzerland, close to the border with France, and its traditional fondue recipe uses a mixture of Gruyère and Emmental cheeses and white wine, with a dash of kirsch.

Neuchâtel fondue

1 garlic clove, peeled

300 ml/1¼ cups dry white wine, such as Neuchâtel, Muscadet or Sauvignon Blanc

400 g/14 oz. Gruyère, coarsely grated

400 g/14 oz. Emmental, coarsely grated

1 tablespoon plain/all-purpose flour

2–4 tablespoons kirsch

freshly ground black pepper

crusty bread, cut into cubes, to serve

fondue pot and tabletop burner

Serves 6

Rub the garlic around the inside of the fondue pot. Pour in the wine and bring it to the boil on the stovetop. Reduce the heat to simmering.

Put the grated cheese in a bowl, add the flour and toss well. Gradually add the cheese mixture to the wine, stirring constantly, and letting each addition melt into the wine. When the mixture is creamy and smooth, add the kirsch and pepper to taste, then transfer the pot to its tabletop burner.

Arrange the bread on serving platters. To eat, spear a piece of bread on a fondue fork, then dip it into the cheese mixture, swirling the fork in a figure of eight to keep the fondue smooth.

Variations

Other Swiss cantons created their own variations of this fondue, usually by substituting their local cheese and wine. Try it with your own local wines and Gruyère-style cheeses.

Fondue Fribourgeois: substitute 400 g/14 oz. Vacherin Fribourgeois, rind removed, finely chopped, for either the Gruyère or Emmental. Italian Fontina is another alternative.

Appenzeller Fondue: Appenzeller is a cheese washed in spiced wine or cider. Use 800 g/1 lb. 12 oz. instead of the Gruyère and Emmental, and a dry German wine or dry cider instead of Neuchâtel. Serve with bread, apples, pears, grapes and chicory.

Comté or Beaufort Fondue: these two French cheeses are big, rich, fruity, Gruyère-types, especially suitable for fondues; substitute 800 g/1 lb. 12 oz. of either.

Rosé Fondue: this is highly unconventional, said to have been invented by tourists in Switzerland who, finding themselves temporarily bereft of white wine, used what they had and came up with a funky pink version. Follow the recipe for Neuchâtel Fondue, substituting a light, dry rosé for the white wine. Not for traditionalists!

A traditional ploughman's lunch is usually made up of a hunk of fresh bread, cheese, ham and pickles, accompanied by an obligatory pint of fine draught beer. This recipe is a homage to those good old days of pub grub eaten around a roaring log fire after a brisk walk in the country. Use a mature Cheddar, or even an aged Cheddar (look for a cheese of around 6 months in age), but make sure it isn't too hard and crumbly.

Ploughman's fondue

1 garlic clove, peeled

500 g/1 lb. 2 oz. mature Cheddar, grated

1 tablespoon plain/all-purpose flour

150 ml/²/₃ cup beer – something with full flavour

30 ml/2 tablespoons organic apple juice

2 teaspoons English mustard

1 teaspoon Worcestershire sauce

a few drops of Tabasco sauce

ham slices, pickled onions, cherry tomatoes, lettuce, radishes, spring onions/scallions, white country loaf, to serve

fondue pot and tabletop burner

Serves 4

Rub the inside of your fondue pot with the garlic clove, reserving any left over for use in another dish. Combine the Cheddar and flour in a bowl, making sure the flour is well dispersed throughout the cheese.

Place the beer and apple juice in the fondue pot on the stovetop and bring to the boil. Simmer for 1 minute, then gradually stir in the cheese mixture until melted. Add the mustard and Worcestershire sauce and continue stirring until you have a lovely creamy consistency. Finally add a few drops of Tabasco.

Transfer the fondue to the tabletop burner and serve with a platter of the ploughman's accompaniments.

Comté has a slightly sharp but nutty taste with a richness and creaminess in the mouth. It is a great choice of cheese for a fondue as it melts so well, and is the preferred cheese in most French fondues. In this recipe the richness is further enhanced by a compote of buttery, caramelized chestnuts, hazelnuts and raisins with fennel seeds, which is somehow reminiscent of Christmas.

Comté with caramelized chestnuts, raisins & hazelnuts

40 g/3 tablespoons butter

30 g/2 tablespoons runny honey

½ teaspoon freshly chopped rosemary, plus extra to garnish

a pinch of fennel seeds, bashed

100 g/3½ oz. whole cooked chestnuts

30 g/¼ cup hazelnuts

30 g/¼ cup raisins

2 tablespoons balsamic vinegar

1 tablespoon cornflour/cornstarch

1 tablespoon freshly squeezed lemon juice

180 ml/¾ cup dry white wine such as Muscadet

500 g/1 lb. 2 oz. Comté, grated

sea salt and freshly ground black pepper

nutty wholemeal loaf, cherry tomatoes and a rocket/arugula salad, to serve

fondue pot and tabletop burner

Serves 4

Place the butter, honey, rosemary and fennel seeds in a frying pan/skillet and heat gently until the butter is melted. Stir in the chestnuts, hazelnuts, raisins and vinegar and cook very gently over a low heat for 5 minutes until gooey and sticky. Season with salt and pepper and keep warm.

To prepare the fondue, stir the cornflour and lemon juice together until smooth. Heat the wine in the fondue pot on the stovetop until boiling. Gradually stir in the cheese, then add the cornflour mixture, stirring until the cheese bubbles. Cook for a few minutes until thickened to your liking.

Transfer the fondue pot to the tabletop burner. Scatter over some fresh rosemary and some of the nuts. Serve with the caramelized compote, chunks of nutty wholemeal bread, some tomatoes and a rocket salad.

Cheddar & Calvados fondue with apple rösti

185 ml/³⁄₄ cup plus 1 tablespoon dry cider

400 g/14 oz. Cheddar, coarsely grated

1 tablespoon plain/all-purpose flour

2–4 tablespoons Calvados

freshly ground black pepper

crispy fried bacon, to serve (optional)

APPLE RÖSTI

3–4 potatoes, about 500 g/1 lb. 2 oz.

2 apples, about 300 g/10½ oz., peeled

freshly squeezed juice of 1 lemon

1 small egg

½ teaspoon sea salt

freshly ground black pepper

1 tablespoon olive oil

fondue pot

Serves 6

To make the rösti, grate the potatoes on the coarse side of a box grater, put into a bowl, cover with water and let soak for 10 minutes. Drain in a colander, then transfer to a clean paper towel and squeeze out very well. Grate the apples into the bowl, add the lemon juice to stop discolouration, toss well, then squeeze out in a paper towel. Put the potato and apple back into a clean dry bowl, add the egg and the salt and pepper and mix well.

Put half the oil into a non-stick frying pan/skillet, around 23 cm/9 inches in diameter, and heat well. Add the potato mixture, press down with a fork and reduce the heat to medium-low. Cook for 10 minutes until brown, loosen with a palette knife, then turn out onto a large plate. Wipe around the pan, add the remaining oil and slide the rösti back into the pan to cook the other side. Cook for a further 10 minutes until cooked through. Keep warm in the oven.

Pour the cider into a fondue pot and bring to the boil. Reduce the heat to simmering. Put the grated cheese and flour into a bowl and toss with a fork. Gradually add the cheese to the pot, stirring constantly, letting each addition melt into the cider. When creamy and smooth, add the Calvados and pepper to taste.

To serve, slice the rösti into 12 wedges, put 2 wedges onto each warmed plate, and top with bacon, if using, and a ladle of the hot fondue.

The flavour combination of pumpkin, Parmesan and sage is a classic of course, but here it is taken to a new level in this roasted pumpkin fondue. You do need to choose a pumpkin that is roughly the same size as the one used here – a smallish pumpkin at 1.75 kg/3¾ lb. or a little either side of that would suffice.

Roasted pumpkin fondue with crispy sage

1 x 1.75 kg/3¾ lb. pumpkin or potimarron

1 tablespoon olive oil

2 garlic cloves, bashed

1 rosemary sprig, bashed

2 tablespoons dry white wine

2 teaspoons cornflour/cornstarch

150 g/5½ oz. Cheddar, grated

150 g/5½ oz. Gruyère or Emmental, grated

75 g/2½ oz. crème fraîche

a little freshly grated nutmeg

30 g/2 tablespoons butter

a small handful of small sage leaves

sea salt and freshly ground black pepper

griddled bread, to serve

roasting pan lined with baking paper

Serves 6

Preheat the oven to 160°C fan/180°C/350°F/Gas 4.

Slice the pumpkin and scoop out and discard the seeds. Drizzle the inside of the pumpkin with oil and season with salt and pepper. Pop the garlic cloves and rosemary sprig into the hollow, replace the lid and transfer to the prepared pan. Roast the pumpkin in the preheated oven for 30 minutes, test for doneness and then keep baking until it is just tender, checking every 15 minutes or so.

Once ready remove the pumpkin from the oven, discard the lid and increase the temperature to 180°C fan/200°C/400°F/Gas 6.

Blend the wine and cornflour together until smooth. Combine the two cheeses and season with a little pepper. Spoon half the cheese mixture into the pumpkin and add the crème fraîche, wine mixture and then the remaining cheeses. Top with some freshly grated nutmeg.

Return the pumpkin to the oven and bake, uncovered, for 25–30 minutes until the cheese is bubbling and lightly golden.

Just before serving, melt the butter in a small saucepan over a medium heat and as soon as the foam dies down, add the sage leaves. Cook for about 2 minutes until the butter is browned and the sage crisp. Pour over the cheese and serve with griddled bread.

Tip: As well as acting as a receptacle for the oozing cheese, you can also scoop out and eat the roasted pumpkin flesh as the level of the melted cheese lowers.

This unbelievably delicious version of the Italian classic fondue uses dried porcini or cep mushrooms for their intensity, making it a year-round option. The dried mushrooms are soaked in hot water until softened, then chopped and added to the cheese along with their delicious soaking water. If you are feeling particularly decadent, serve it drizzled with a little truffle oil or even freshly sliced black truffles when available. Best served simply with a little bread, the fonduta could also be accompanied by a side salad.

Porcini fonduta

500 g/1 lb. 2 oz. Fontina or Fontal, finely diced

300 ml/1¼ cups full-fat/whole milk

30 g/1 oz. dried porcini mushrooms

225 ml/1 cup boiling water

1 garlic clove, finely chopped

50 g/3½ tablespoons butter, softened

5 large egg yolks

truffle oil (optional)

sea salt and freshly ground black pepper

Italian-style bread, to serve

fondue pot

Serves 6

Place the sliced cheese in a shallow dish and pour over the milk. Leave to soak for at least 1 hour to help the cheese absorb the milk.

Meanwhile, place the porcini in a bowl and pour over the boiling water. Leave to soak for 30 minutes. Drain the mushrooms over a small saucepan to retain the liquid, then finely chop the mushrooms. Place the chopped mushrooms and garlic into the pan with the mushroom liquid and bring to a simmer. Cook for 10–15 minutes until the mushrooms are really tender and most of the liquid absorbed. Season to taste and set aside to cool.

Pour the milk and cheese into a fondue pot and place this over a saucepan of just simmering water (make sure that the base of the pot does not make contact with the water). Stir the milk and cheese over the heat until the cheese is completely melted. Gradually beat in the butter and remove the pan from the heat, then gradually beat in the egg yolks, one at a time, stirring constantly.

Return the pan to the heat and beat constantly until the mixture thickens and becomes homogeneous. Do not allow the cheese mixture to boil at any point or it will curdle. As soon as it is creamy, stir in the reserved mushrooms and any remaining liquid, then season to taste.

Transfer the fondue pot to the table (do not place on a tabletop burner, but do use a heatproof mat) and, if using, drizzle over a little truffle oil. Serve with hunks of country-style Italian bread.

This is such a simple yet delicious appetizer. If you can't find green ginger wine, use sherry instead and increase the quantity of fresh ginger to 1 tablespoon. You could also serve this as a dip at parties – just make sure the burner and pot are safely fixed on the serving platter.

Ginger & crab fondue

25 g/¼ cup toasted flaked/slivered almonds or 50 g/⅜ cup Brazil nuts

250 g/1 heaped cup cream cheese

4 tablespoons green ginger wine

4 spring onions/scallions, finely sliced

2 teaspoons grated fresh ginger

175 g/6 oz. cooked crab meat

crackers, breadsticks, grissini or toast, cut into strips or triangles, to serve

fondue pot and tabletop burner

**Serves 8
as an appetizer**

If using Brazil nuts, use a mandoline or vegetable peeler to finely slice them into shavings. Set aside.

Put the cream cheese and ginger wine into a fondue pot and stir until smooth. Add the spring onions and grated ginger and heat gently on the stovetop until bubbling. Stir in the crab meat, then scatter over the toasted almonds or Brazil nut shavings.

Transfer the pot to its tabletop burner to keep warm and serve with crackers, breadsticks, grissini or toast alongside for dipping.

Fondues don't have to be Swiss — they are also a fabulously easy way to throw a North African-themed dinner party. Serve platters of couscous tossed with herbs and sautéed vegetables, pass around bowls of relish, then have your guests cook their own chicken and duck skewers. The rendered duck fat added to the cooking oil gives a wonderful depth to the dish.

Chicken & duck fondue with Tunisian relish

500 g/1 lb. 2 oz. skinless, boneless chicken breasts or thighs

500 g/1 lb. 2 oz. duck breast, with the fat trimmed and reserved

750 ml–1.25 litres/3¼–5 cups peanut or safflower oil

cooked couscous tossed with pomegranate seeds, pistachio nuts and coriander/cilantro and steamed carrots, to serve

TUNISIAN RELISH

4 large tomatoes, skinned and deseeded

peel of 1 preserved lemon

2 tablespoons harissa or tomato purée/paste

a large handful of fresh coriander/cilantro, chopped

2 tablespoons olive oil

sea salt

fondue pot and tabletop burner

Serves 6

To make the Tunisian relish, chop the tomatoes and preserved lemon peel very finely and put into a bowl. Stir in the harissa or tomato purée, coriander and olive oil. Season with salt and set aside for a few hours to allow the flavours to develop.

Cut the chicken and duck into 1-cm/½-inch strips and thread strips of each onto the skewers, about 50 g/1¾ oz. per skewer, leaving about 4 cm/1½ inches clear at the end, so the skewer can rest on the bottom of the pot without sticking. Arrange on a serving platter. Set platters of couscous and bowls of relish on the table.

Fill a metal fondue pot one-third full with oil and add the duck fat trimmings. Heat the oil to 180°C/350°F or until a cube of bread browns in 40 seconds. Very carefully transfer the pot to its tabletop burner. Remove the duck fat when it becomes brown.

Invite guests to cook the skewers of duck and chicken in the hot oil for 2 minutes or until cooked through, then eat with the couscous and relish.

Lamb makes a great variation on the classic beef fondue. To make the lamb easier to slice, freeze it for about 1 hour first. Baharat is a fragrant Middle Eastern spice mix – it can be a combination of many herbs, spices and flowers, and here nuts have been added to soften the blend.

Lamb fondue with toasted baharat

1.25 kg/2¾ lb. lamb fillet, thinly sliced

750 ml–1.25 litres/3¼–5 cups peanut or safflower oil

flatbreads, hummus, salad leaves and plain yogurt, to serve (optional)

BAHARAT SPICE MIX

125 g/1 cup blanched almonds

125 g/1 cup shelled pistachios

4 tablespoons sesame seeds

1 tablespoon black peppercorns

1½ tablespoons cumin seeds

1 tablespoon coriander seeds

2 cinnamon sticks, crumbled

1–2 tablespoons sweet paprika

½ teaspoon grated nutmeg

fondue pot and tabletop burner

Serves 6

To make the baharat, put the almonds and pistachios into a dry frying pan/skillet and toast for a few minutes until brown. Let cool, then transfer to a food processor and grind coarsely. Toast the sesame seeds in the pan, then add to the processor and pulse briefly. Put the black peppercorns, cumin, coriander and crumbled cinnamon into the pan and dry-toast for a few minutes until fragrant. Transfer to a spice grinder, add the paprika and nutmeg and grind to a powder. Alternatively, use a mortar and pestle. Transfer to a sterilized jar, add the nut and seed mixture and shake well. The mixture will keep for 1 month, and can be used to flavour meats or vegetables, or as a dip with bread and oil.

To prepare the fondue, pat the lamb dry with paper towels and arrange on a serving platter. Spoon the baharat into 6 small bowls.

Fill a metal fondue pot one-third full with oil. Heat the oil on the stovetop until it reaches 190°C/375°F or until a cube of bread browns in 30 seconds. Very carefully transfer the pot to its tabletop burner. Invite each guest to thread a piece of lamb onto a skewer and dip into the hot oil for about 15–30 seconds. Dip the hot lamb into the baharat, then eat. Alternatively, make flatbread wraps with the lamb, hummus, salad and yogurt.

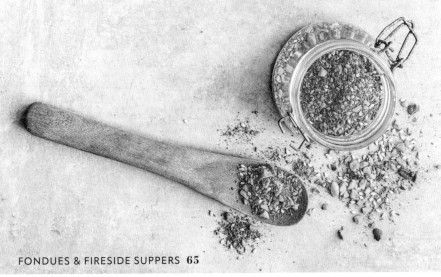

Raclette is an essential experience for all cheese lovers. Traditionally, huge half wheels of Raclette are heated beside an open fire. Periodically, the melted layer is scraped onto a plate and served with potatoes, pickled onions and cornichons. Nowadays, special equipment is available for melting the cheese, ranging from large grills holding two halves of a wheel, to nifty tabletop versions with little grill pans for individual servings. If you don't own one, an ordinary grill/broiler and pieces of non-stick baking paper work very well too.

Classic Raclette

100 g/3½ oz. Raclette, or other melting cheese, cut into 4 slices

200 g/7 oz. new potatoes, boiled in their skins

8–12 cornichons

8–12 silverskin/cocktail onions

raclette mahine

Serves 1

Preheat the raclette machine, if using, according to the manufacturer's instructions. Warm a serving plate in a low oven. Arrange a platter of potatoes, cornichons and silverskin onions on the table.

Place a slice of cheese into one of the small raclette trays, heat until melted, then eat with the accompaniments.

Tip: This recipe is easily duplicated for any number of guests.

Variation

If you don't have a raclette machine, heat a conventional grill/broiler until very hot and put 4 slices of cheese onto 4 pieces of baking paper, 12 cm/5 inch square. When your guests are seated and ready, grill/broil the cheese for about 2 minutes until bubbling. Using a metal spatula, scrape the cheese off the paper onto a warm plate and serve as before.

In France, a brandade is a thick, creamy purée made with salt cod. With a few alterations, it makes a wonderful fondue. Because preparing salt cod can be a time-consuming business, this recipe uses a smoked fish – not traditional but still good. Serve it in a fondue pot or in individual dishes.

Individual smoked fish fondues

750 g/1 lb. 10 oz. smoked fish, such
  as cod or haddock, skinned and
  cut into cubes
2 garlic cloves, crushed
125 ml/½ cup extra virgin olive oil
225 g/1 cup cream cheese
125 ml/½ cup full-fat/whole milk
2 tablespoons freshly squeezed
  lemon juice
2 tablespoons freshly grated Parmesan
cayenne pepper
sea salt and freshly ground
  black pepper

TO SERVE

8 eggs, soft-boiled/cooked and halved
strips of toast
8 small ramekins, buttered

Serves 8

Preheat the oven to 160°C fan/180°C/350°F/Gas 4.

Put the flaked fish and garlic into a food processor or blender. With the motor running, pour in the olive oil to form a paste. Add the cream cheese and pulse until just mixed.

Stir in the milk and lemon juice. Taste, then season with salt and pepper (take care, because the fish is often quite salty). Spoon into the 8 buttered ramekins and scatter over the Parmesan and a little cayenne pepper.

Bake in the preheated oven for about 20 minutes until hot and bubbly. Serve with the eggs and toast for dipping.

Tip: To serve the smoked fish fondue in a pot, transfer the mixture from the food processor to the pot once you have added the cream cheese, and heat gently, stirring. Add the milk, then the lemon juice. Transfer the pot to the tabletop burner to keep warm. If the mixture is too thick, add a splash of dry white wine. Serve as in the main recipe.

Similar to Southern India's dosas, this pancake base uses rice, first soaked for a few hours, and then left overnight. As it soaks, it gently ferments which adds a delicate flavour and a little bubble to the mixture. Served alongside spiced potatoes, there are enough warming spices included here to heat up any cold winter evening.

Rice pancakes with spiced potatoes

300 g/2¼ cups rice flour

100 g/generous ½ cup part urad dal (split black lentils)

1 teaspoon fenugreek seeds

50 g/2 oz. ghee

sea salt

SPICED POTATOES

800 g/1¾ lb. potatoes, peeled and cut into 3-cm/1¼-inch pieces

60 ml/¼ cup vegetable oil

1 onion, finely chopped

a thumb-sized piece of fresh ginger, grated

2 garlic cloves, finely chopped

5 fresh curry leaves

1 teaspoon mustard seeds

1 teaspoon ground coriander

1 teaspoon ground turmeric

30 g/1 oz. mixed coriander/cilantro and mint, leaves picked

1 long green chilli/chile, finely chopped

sea salt and freshly ground black pepper

TO SERVE

grated coconut

sliced green chilli/chile

chilli/chili powder

tamarind chutney

lime wedges, for squeezing

Serves 4–6

Place the rice flour in a bowl, add just enough cold water to cover and leave to soak for 2–3 hours.

Rinse the urad dal, place in a bowl with enough cold water to cover them and soak for 2–3 hours. Drain the lentils, then place in an electric blender and grind, adding just enough water to form a thick fine paste.

Mix the ground lentil paste with the soaked rice flour until you get a thick batter. Add salt to taste and leave the batter in a warm place overnight to ferment.

The next morning, make the spiced potatoes. Cook the potatoes in a saucepan of simmering salted water for 25–30 minutes until tender, then drain well and set aside. Heat the oil in a large frying pan/skillet, add the onion, ginger, garlic and curry leaves and cook for 7–8 minutes until the onion is soft, then add spices and stir until fragrant. Add the potatoes and 80 ml/⅓ cup water, cover and simmer for 3–5 minutes for the flavours to combine and the potatoes are very soft. Stir in the coriander, mint and green chilli and season to taste.

Mix the batter thoroughly again, and stir through the fenugreek seeds – it should be a thin pancake consistency (add water if it's too thick). Add a little ghee to a frying pan/skillet until it is hot. Pour a ladleful of the batter into the centre and spread evenly in circles until it reaches the edges of the pan. Fry for 2–3 minutes per side, turning once, until golden and crisp. Wipe out the pan with paper towels and repeat with remaining ghee and batter. Top the pancakes with the spiced potatoes, coconut, green chilli and chilli powder and serve with tamarind chutney and lime wedges for squeezing.

Butternut squash is a perfect winter ingredient, especially once it's baked in the oven to bring out its natural sweetness. When paired with the warming spices of zhoug, it makes for an essential winter dish to enjoy in front of a roaring fire.

Butternut squash with eggs, cavolo nero, feta & jalapeño zhoug

500 g/1 lb. 2 oz. peeled and deseeded butternut squash, cut into 2.5-cm/1-inch chunks

1 tablespoon olive oil, plus extra for roasting the butternut squash and cavolo nero

2 small garlic cloves, crushed

1 teaspoon thyme leaves

30 g/3 tablespoons whole almonds, toasted and roughly chopped

a few sprigs of fresh mint, leaves roughly chopped

1 teaspoon pomegranate molasses

6 stems cavolo nero (approx. 70 g/ 2½ oz.), stalks removed, chopped into 2.5-cm/1-inch pieces

2 slices of focaccia or pitta bread

2 eggs

50 g/⅓ cup feta cheese, crumbled

1–2 tablespoons pomegranate seeds

sea salt and freshly ground black pepper

JALAPEÑO ZHOUG

65 g/3 cups coriander/cilantro, leaves and stalks chopped

30 g/½ cup jalapeño or green chillies/ chiles, chopped

1 teaspoon sea salt

1 garlic clove, chopped

200 ml/¾ cup olive oil

20 ml/1 tablespoon plus 1 teaspoon freshly squeezed lemon juice

2 baking sheets lined with baking parchment

Serves 2

Preheat the oven to 160°C fan/180°C/350°F/Gas 4.

Spread the butternut squash chunks out on a prepared baking sheet, drizzle with olive oil, season with salt and pepper and roast in the preheated oven for about 20 minutes or until tender. Remove from the oven, transfer to a bowl and mash roughly with a fork, keeping it a bit chunky.

Heat 1 tablespoon olive oil in a small pan, add the crushed garlic and thyme leaves and cook over a gentle heat for a couple of minutes. Add this to the smashed butternut squash with the chopped almonds, mint and pomegranate molasses. Season with salt and pepper.

Put the cavolo nero in a bowl, drizzle with olive oil and season with salt and pepper. Gently rub the oil into the cavolo nero with your fingers and spread it out on the second prepared baking sheet. Roast on the top shelf of the preheated oven for about 5 minutes until crispy.

To make the Jalapeño Zhoug, put all the ingredients in a food processor or blender and blitz to a paste.

When ready to serve, gently reheat the smashed butternut squash in a pan. Toast the focaccia or pitta bread and poach the eggs. Heap the smashed butternut squash on two plates, top with the crumbled feta, cavolo nero and pomegranate seeds. Serve with a generous dollop of Zhoug, the toasted focaccia and a poached egg.

If anything epitomizes an indulgent cold weather brunch, it's got to be a combination of flaked smoked haddock, topped with a poached egg and a blanket of slightly sharp yet creamy sauce. Here, the poaching milk from the fish is used to create a light but no less delicious faux hollandaise.

Smoked haddock on sourdough

400 g/14 oz. smoked, undyed haddock

about 500 ml/2 cups full-fat/
  whole milk

1 dried bay leaf

4 slices of sourdough bread

a generous pinch of dried chilli/hot
  red pepper flakes (optional)

12 spears fresh asparagus

1 tablespoon butter

1 tablespoon plain/all-purpose flour

½ teaspoon English/hot mustard

½ teaspoon cider vinegar

4 eggs, or 12 quail's eggs, as preferred

freshly chopped flat-leaf parsley,
  to garnish

sea salt and freshly ground
  black pepper

olive oil, for brushing

Serves 4

Put the haddock in a snug-fitting saucepan and pour in enough milk to cover. Add a few grinds of black pepper and the bay leaf. Poach on a low simmer for about 5 minutes, until the flesh is opaque. Leave the fish in the milk until cool before removing it. Set aside and reserve the poaching milk.

Brush the sourdough bread with olive oil, season and sprinkle with a pinch of dried chilli flakes, if using. Lightly oil the asparagus. Heat a griddle/grill pan until really hot. Add the bread and toast for 2 minutes on each side, warming the asparagus in the pan at the same time until lightly browned and nutty.

Set a small saucepan over a low heat. Add the butter and flour and heat for 2 minutes or so to cook out the flour, then whisk in 125 ml/½ cup of the reserved poaching milk. Bring to a simmer, continuously whisking until you have a smooth, creamy sauce, adding more milk to achieve your desired consistency. Add the mustard and vinegar, stir, taste for seasoning and set to one side until needed.

To poach the eggs, bring a small saucepan of water to a simmer, swirl the water, then slide an egg out of its shell and into the centre. Poach for about 5 minutes until the white is cooked, then carefully remove with a slotted spoon and drain on paper towels (if using quail's eggs, only for 1–2 minutes). You may need to poach the eggs in batches.

Place the toasted sourdough slices on a serving board with the flaked fish and asparagus arranged on top, add the soft poached eggs and pour over as much faux hollandaise sauce as you fancy. Sprinkle some freshly chopped parsley over the top to garnish and add a grinding or two of black pepper.

A savoury cheesecake mixture, or if you like, a cheesy custard, is poured over slices of day-old baguette and baked until firm and golden. The richness and heartiness of the dish is perfectly offset by the tangy beetroot/beet relish. A side of green salad is the ideal accompaniment.

Baked savoury bread & four-cheese pudding with beetroot jam

50 g/3½ tablespoons butter, plus extra for greasing

2 leeks, trimmed and thinly sliced

1 garlic clove, crushed

1 teaspoon freshly chopped thyme

350 g/1½ cups cream cheese

250 g/1¼ cups crème fraîche

500 ml/2 cups full-fat/whole milk

4 eggs, beaten

75 g/generous ¾ cup grated Cheddar or Gruyère

50 g/scant ½ cup Gorgonzola or Roquefort, crumbled

a little freshly grated nutmeg

1 medium baguette (about 35 cm/14 inches in length)

2 tablespoons grated Parmesan

sea salt and freshly ground black pepper

green salad, to serve (optional)

BEETROOT JAM

200 g/7 oz. raw beetroot/beets, peeled and grated

1 small onion, thinly sliced

100 ml/⅔ cup red wine vinegar

100 g/½ cup dark soft brown sugar

1 teaspoon sea salt

4 x 250-ml/9-oz. (or a 2–3-litre/quart) Dutch ovens

Serves 4

Start by making the beetroot jam. Place all the ingredients in a saucepan with 60 ml/¼ cup water, bring to the boil and simmer over a medium-low heat for 25–30 minutes or until the liquid has evaporated and the mixture is slightly sticky. Set aside to cool.

Melt the butter in a frying pan/skillet over a medium heat and gently fry the leeks, garlic, thyme and salt and pepper for 5–6 minutes until softened. Remove from the heat.

Lightly butter the Dutch ovens. In a bowl, beat together the cream cheese, crème fraîche, milk and eggs until smooth. Stir in the Cheddar, Gorgonzola, nutmeg, cooled leeks and a little salt and pepper.

Cut the baguette into 1-cm/½-inch thick slices, divide between the prepared pans and pour the cheese custard over the top, pressing the bread slices down into the pans. Set aside for 30 minutes to soak.

Preheat the oven to 180°C fan/200°C/400°F/Gas 6.

Scatter each pudding with a little of the grated Parmesan and transfer the pans to the preheated oven. Bake for about 30–35 minutes (or 50–60 minutes for a large pudding) or until the puddings are puffed up and golden. Cover the pans after about 25 minutes if the tops are becoming too brown. Test with a skewer inserted into a pudding – it is cooked when the skewer comes out clean.

Remove from the oven and allow to sit for 5 minutes. Serve with the beetroot jam and a crisp green salad.

If you are hesitant to cook cheese soufflés, this is the recipe for you. Found on bistro menus throughout France, the soufflés are baked, cooled, turned out and re-baked with a creamy sauce. This is one of the most delicious cheese dishes you will ever eat — magically rich but light, and warming for the soul.

Twice-baked cheese soufflés with beaufort cream

olive oil, for greasing

3 tablespoons dried breadcrumbs

60 g/4 tablespoons butter

75 g/½ cup plus 1 tablespoon plain/all-purpose flour

½ teaspoon Dijon mustard

500 ml/2 cups full-fat/whole milk

150 g/5½ oz. semi-soft goat's cheese log, diced

50 g/1¾ oz. Parmesan, finely grated

4 large/extra large eggs, separated

400 ml/1¾ cups double/heavy cream

100 g/3½ oz. Beaufort, grated

sea salt and freshly ground black pepper

green salad, to serve

8 x 180-ml/¾-cup ramekin dishes

8 x individual gratin dishes, about 14 cm/5½ in. across

Serves 8

Preheat the oven to 160°C fan/180°C/350°F/Gas 4. Lightly grease the ramekin dishes with a little olive oil and then dust the insides with breadcrumbs to coat. Transfer the ramekins to a deep baking pan.

Melt the butter in a small pan, add the flour and mustard, season with salt and pepper and stir well with a wooden spoon over a low heat until the mixture comes together. Continue to cook, stirring, for 1 minute. Remove the pan from the heat and gradually whisk in the milk. Return to the heat and stir until it comes to the boil. Simmer gently for 2 minutes, stirring, until the sauce has thickened. Cool for 5 minutes, then beat in the goat's cheese and 30 g/1 oz. of the Parmesan until melted. Beat in the egg yolks one at a time and transfer the mixture to a large bowl.

Whisk the egg whites in a separate clean bowl until soft peaks form, then fold into the cheese mixture until evenly incorporated. Divide the mixture between the prepared ramekins and run a knife around the edges to encourage the rise. Pour boiling water into the baking pan to come halfway up the sides of the ramekins and bake in the preheated oven for 20–25 minutes or until risen and browned. Remove the soufflés from the oven and leave to cool for at least 30 minutes.

Oil the gratin dishes. Run a small palette knife around the edges of each soufflé and turn them out, placing them upside down in the prepared dishes. Heat the cream in a small saucepan until it just boils, pour over and around the soufflés, then carefully sprinkle over the Beaufort and the remaining Parmesan. Return to the preheated oven and bake for a further 10–15 minutes until bubbling and golden. Serve with a green salad.

The Reblochon in this classic winter warmer, originating in south-eastern France, can be diced, sliced, quartered or left whole as was originally intended, atop the creamy potato and bacon mixture underneath. To be honest, it works any which way!

Tartiflette

500 g/1 lb. 2 oz. potatoes, such as Charlotte, halved

150 g/5½ oz. smoked bacon lardons

50 g/3½ tablespoons butter, plus extra for greasing

1 onion, sliced

1 garlic clove, sliced

2 teaspoons freshly chopped thyme

400 ml/1¾ cups crème fraîche

500 g/1 lb. 2 oz. Reblochon, cut into quarters

sea salt and freshly ground black pepper

chunks of bread and a green salad, to serve

a 1.5 litre/quart baking dish

Serves 6

Preheat the oven to 180°C fan/200°C/400°F/Gas 6 and lightly butter the baking dish.

Cook the potatoes in a pan of boiling water for 12–15 minutes until just tender, then drain and shake dry.

Place a large frying pan/skillet over a low heat, add the lardons and heat gently until all the fat is rendered down in the pan. Increase the heat to high and fry until browned, then remove with a slotted spoon. Add half the butter and the potatoes to the pan and fry for 5 minutes until lightly golden. Transfer to the prepared dish, add the lardons and stir to combine.

Add the remaining butter to the frying pan and fry the onion, garlic, thyme and a little salt and pepper over a medium heat for 5 minutes until softened. Stir in the crème fraîche and bring to the boil, then immediately pour the cream mixture over the potatoes.

Arrange the cheese on top, transfer to the preheated oven and bake uncovered for 20–30 minutes, or until golden and bubbling. Serve with bread to mop up the juices and a crisp green salad on the side.

Warming one-pots & pies

A classic Hungarian stew topped with cornbread dumplings makes this a complete one-pot meal. The richness of the sauce is enhanced by the paprika.

Hungarian goulash with cornbread dumplings

90 ml/6 tablespoons olive oil

1.5 kg/3¼ lb. braising or chuck steak, cubed into 2-cm/¾-inch pieces

2 onions, thinly sliced

2 red (bell) peppers, seeded and roughly chopped

2 garlic cloves, finely chopped

1 tablespoon sweet or smoked paprika, plus extra to dust

2 teaspoons caraway seeds

1.25 litres/5 cups beef or chicken stock

4 tablespoons tomato purée/paste

sea salt and freshly ground black pepper

sour cream or crème fraîche, to serve

CORNBREAD DUMPLINGS

150 g/1 cup plus 2 tablespoons plain/all-purpose flour

1 tablespoon baking powder

a pinch cayenne pepper

150 g/1 cup instant polenta/cornmeal

50 g/½ cup finely grated Cheddar

1 tablespoon freshly chopped flat-leaf parsley

250 ml/1 cup buttermilk

a 5–6-litre/quart Dutch oven

Serves 4–6

Preheat the oven to 160°C fan/180°C/350°F/Gas 4.

Heat half the oil in the Dutch oven and fry the beef, in batches if needed, for 5 minutes until browned on all sides. Remove from the pan with a slotted spoon. Add the remaining oil and fry the onions, peppers and garlic for 5 minutes, then stir in the paprika, caraway seeds and a little salt and pepper. Fry for a further 5 minutes until the onions and peppers are well softened.

Return the beef to the pan, add the stock and tomato purée, stirring well, and bring to the boil. Cover the pan and transfer it to the preheated oven. Bake for 2 hours, or until the beef is tender.

Make the dumplings. Sift the flour, baking powder and cayenne pepper into a bowl and stir in the polenta, cheese, parsley and a little salt and pepper. Make a well in the middle and add the buttermilk. Work together to make a soft dough.

Remove the pan from the oven and the lid from the pan. Carefully spoon in 12 dollops of the dumpling mixture to cover the meat (but leave gaps in between each one). Cover with the lid and return the pan to the oven. Cook for 15–20 minutes or until the dumplings are puffed up. Check they are cooked by inserting a skewer into the middle – it should come out clean; if not, cook for a further 5 minutes until ready.

Serve the goulash accompanied by some sour cream or crème fraîche and a dusting of paprika, if wished.

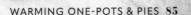

Moroccan lamb with dates & olives

6 small lamb shanks (or lamb neck chops), about 1.5 kg/3¼ lb. in total

2 onions, roughly chopped

2 red (bell) peppers, seeded and roughly chopped

4 garlic cloves, chopped

4 sprigs of fresh rosemary, bashed

1 orange, thickly sliced

2 cinnamon sticks, bashed

750-ml bottle red wine

2 tablespoons olive oil

1 tablespoon ras el hanout (see below)

400-g/14-oz can chopped tomatoes

2 tablespoons date syrup or molasses

125 g/4½ oz. small stoned/pitted black olives

75 g/2½ oz. dates, stoned/pitted and chopped

4 tablespoons freshly chopped coriander/cilantro

sea salt and freshly ground black pepper

couscous, coriander/cilantro and pomegranate seeds, to serve

RAS EL HANOUT

3 cardamom pods, seeds only

1 teaspoon coriander seeds

½ teaspoon cumin seeds

½ teaspoon sweet paprika

½ teaspoon ground cinnamon

½ teaspoon ground cayenne

½ teaspoons ground turmeric

½ teaspoon ground ginger

6-litre/quart Dutch oven

Serves 6

A day ahead, place the lamb shanks in a large ceramic bowl or plastic container. Add the onions, peppers, garlic, rosemary, orange slices, cinnamon sticks and some salt and pepper. Pour over the wine and leave to marinate overnight in the fridge.

Make the ras el hanout. Place the cardamom seeds, coriander seeds and cumin seeds in a small dry frying pan/skillet and place over a medium heat. Cook for 2–3 minutes until they are browned and starting to release their aroma. Let cool, then grind to a fine powder in a spice grinder (or a mortar and pestle). Mix with the powdered spices and store in a jar until required.

The next day, strain the marinade juices into a jug/pitcher, reserving all the vegetables and set both aside. Pat the lamb shanks dry with paper towels and season generously with salt and pepper.

Heat half the oil in the Dutch oven over a high heat. Fry the shanks for 5 minutes until browned all over. Remove with a slotted spoon and reduce the heat to medium. Add the remaining oil and the reserved vegetables to the pan (but not the orange slices) and fry for 5–6 minutes over a medium heat until browned and sticky. Stir in the ras el hanout spice mix, stir for 1 minute.

Return the lamb to the pan with the orange slices, the marinade juices, tomatoes and date syrup, stirring well. Bring the stew to the boil, cover, reduce the heat, and simmer over a very low heat for 2 hours until the lamb is starting to fall from the bone. Remove the lid, stir in the olives and dates and cook uncovered for a further 15 minutes until the sauce has thickened. Stir in the coriander and adjust seasoning to taste.

Serve with the couscous, herbs and pomegranate seeds.

Many Vietnamese dishes pair meat or fish with a sweet caramel sauce to balance the saltiness of fish sauce, the fire of chillies/chiles, and the sharpness of lime juice. Add in Japanese miso and red wine, and you have a truly global dish. Beef cheeks need a long cooking time before they soften to mouthwatering tenderness in this winter warmer.

Vietnamese-style miso, red wine & caramel beef cheeks

1.5 kg/3¼ lb. beef cheeks

500 ml/2 cups beef stock

500 ml/2 cups red wine

250 g/1¼ cups caster/granulated sugar

4 tablespoons brown miso paste

60 ml/4 tablespoons fish sauce

1 tablespoon light soy sauce

4 garlic cloves, bashed

5-cm/2-inch piece of root ginger, peeled and bashed

2 whole star anise, lightly bruised

2 cinnamon sticks, lightly bruised

jasmine rice, to serve

PICKLES

2 tablespoons fresh lime juice

1 tablespoon fish sauce

1 tablespoon sugar

2 carrots, trimmed and thinly sliced

1 courgette/zucchini, trimmed and thinly sliced

½ cucumber, seeded and thinly sliced

a few fresh mint and coriander/ cilantro leaves

1 red chilli/chile, sliced (optional)

a 4–5-litre/quart Dutch oven

Serves 8

Preheat the oven to 130°C fan/150°C/300°F/Gas 2.

Wash and dry the beef cheeks and then cut into 5-cm/2-inch pieces. Place in the Dutch oven, cover with cold water, bring to the boil and cook for 5 minutes, skimming all the scum from the surface. Drain and discard the water, wipe the pan clean and return the beef to the pan. Add the stock and wine to the pan and bring to the boil.

Meanwhile, place the sugar in a small saucepan 125 ml/½ cup water. Bring to the boil and simmer for 8–10 minutes without stirring, until the liquid starts to caramelize and turn a golden brown. Immediately stir the caramel sauce into the stock.

Combine the miso, fish sauce and soy sauce until smooth and stir into the pan along with the garlic, ginger, star anise and cinnamon sticks. Return to the boil and place a sheet of parchment paper over the surface of the stew. Cover the pan with the lid and transfer to the preheated oven. Cook for 4–5 hours, checking after 4 hours to see how the meat is cooking – it should be falling apart and the juices should be starting to thicken.

About 30 minutes before the beef is ready, make the vegetable pickles. Combine the lime juice, fish sauce and sugar, stirring to dissolve the sugar. Mix the sliced vegetables together in a bowl, pour the lime mixture over the top and stir well. Add the herbs and chilli, if using.

Using a slotted spoon, transfer the beef cheeks to a warmed platter. Place the pan on the stovetop, bring the pan juices to a simmer and cook for 5 minutes until the sauce is glossy and thickened. Pour the meat juices over the beef cheeks and serve with the pickles and some jasmine rice.

The original recipe for baked beans dates back to the early days of American food culture. Beans were a staple food of native Americans, who cooked them in a sauce and ate them with a type of cornbread. It is thought that early Dutch settlers, arriving into Boston, brought their braadpans (Dutch ovens) with them and these great cooking pots soon found their way into American kitchens. This is generally considered to be how this dish got its name.

Boston baked beans

350 g/2 cups dried haricot/navy beans

500 g/1 lb. 2 oz gammon knuckle

½ teaspoon bicarbonate of soda/
 baking soda

1 garlic clove, crushed

1 onion, finely chopped

500 ml/2 cups passata/strained
 tomatoes

2 tablespoons tomato purée/paste

125 g/⅓ cup molasses or black treacle

1 tablespoon Dijon mustard

1 tablespoon red wine vinegar

a few drops of Tabasco sauce

sea salt and freshly ground
 black pepper

toasted bread, to serve

freshly chopped flat-leaf parsley
 (optional)

a 6-litre/quart Dutch oven

Serves 4–6

A day ahead, place the beans in a large bowl and cover with cold water. Place the gammon in a second bowl (or large pan) and cover with cold water. Leave both to soak overnight. The next day, drain them both.

Preheat the oven to 130°C fan/150°C/300°F/Gas 2.

Place the beans in the Dutch oven and add enough water to cover them by a good 10 cm/4 inches. Add the bicarbonate of soda and bring to a rolling boil. Cook fast for 10 minutes, then strain the beans and reserve 750 ml/3 cups of the cooking liquid.

Return the drained beans and the reserved liquid to the Dutch oven and add all the remaining ingredients, including the gammon, plus a little salt and pepper. Bring to the boil, cover, and transfer the pan to the preheated oven. Bake for 2½ hours, then check the level of the liquid, add a little more if the dish is dry, and continue to cook for a further 30 minutes until the beans and gammon are tender.

Carefully remove the skin, bone and fat from the gammon and as soon as you can, shred the meat. Season the beans to taste with a little more salt and pepper. Serve the beans and shredded gammon with toasted bread, scattered with a little parsley, if wished.

Oxtail stew with dumplings

1.5–2 kg/3¼–4½ lb. oxtail

olive oil, for frying

1 large onion, diced

1 large leek, diced

1 celery stick/rib, diced

a 5-cm/2 in. piece of ginger, cut into 1.5-cm/½-in. slices

50 g/heaping ⅓ cup plain/all-purpose flour

500 ml/2 cups red wine

1 large carrot, thickly sliced

3 star anise

2 bay leaves

60 ml/¼ cup dark soy sauce

a pinch of cayenne pepper

1 tablespoon smoked paprika

60 g/⅓ cup brown sugar

1 tablespoon white wine vinegar or cider vinegar

a small bunch of coriander/cilantro

1 litre/4 cups beef stock

1 garlic bulb, halved widthways

sea salt and freshly ground black pepper

mashed potatoes, to serve

DUMPLINGS

200 g/1½ cups self-raising/rising flour

100 g/7 tablespoons cold butter, grated

80 ml/⅓ cup full-fat/whole milk

a 4-litre/quart Dutch oven

Serves 4

Preheat the oven to 160°C fan/180°C/350°F/Gas 4.

Season the oxtails very generously with salt and pepper. Heat the Dutch oven without oil, add the oxtails and brown them all over (you may need to do this in batches) until they form a dark crust. Remove from the pan.

Reduce the heat to medium (add a splash of olive oil now if needed) and sauté the onion, leek and celery for about 5 minutes until the onion is caramelized. Add the ginger and, after 30 seconds, stir in the flour and cook for a further minute. Pour in the red wine, stirring as you do (don't worry about lumps; they'll dissolve during cooking) and simmer to reduce the liquid by half. Add all the remaining ingredients, except the coriander, beef stock and garlic.

Cut the bunch of coriander about halfway down, just where the leaves stop. Save the leaves to garnish, chop the stalks and add to the pot. Return the oxtails to the pot, including any juices, and pour over enough beef stock to cover. Add the halved garlic bulb and bring to the boil, cover with foil and then a tight-fitting lid (if it's not tight fitting it will dry out) and bake in the preheated oven for 5 hours (check it halfway through in case you need to add more hot water).

Meanwhile, make the dumplings. In a large mixing bowl, combine the flour and butter and lightly season with salt and pepper. Work the mixture with your fingertips until you have a scraggy mess, then add the milk and keep kneading until it all comes together; it's OK if it's a bit wet. Take a ping-pong ball-sized portion, roll in your hands to form a ball and flatten slightly, continue until all the dough is used; you'll get about 10 pieces. You can chill these until you're ready.

With 20 minutes left of cooking; remove the dish from the oven and increase the oven temperature to 180°C fan/200°C/400°F/Gas 6. Place the dumplings on top of the meat/liquid (with space around each one), cover the pan again with just the lid and return to the oven for 20 minutes. Remove from the oven and leave to rest for 10 minutes before serving in bowls, garnished with coriander.

This is an Italian pasta and bean dish (fagioli meaning bean in Italian), cooked in a rich tomato sauce and served topped with grated Parmesan. It is a hearty dish, more a stew than a soup. As well as a good grating of fresh Parmesan, it is lovely drizzled with a fruity extra virgin olive oil. Start this recipe a day ahead.

Pasta e fagioli

200 g/1¼ cups dried borlotti/
  cranberry or haricot/cannellini
  beans

2 onions

1 bay leaf

60 ml/4 tablespoons extra virgin
  olive oil

150 g/5½ oz. pancetta or smoked
  bacon, rind removed, diced

1 large carrot, diced

1 large potato, diced

2 sticks/ribs of celery, diced

2 garlic cloves, finely chopped

2 teaspoons freshly chopped thyme

1 teaspoon freshly chopped rosemary

400-g/14-oz. can passata/strained
  tomatoes

2 tablespoons tomato purée/paste

200 g/7 oz. small conchiglie
  or ditali pasta

1–2 tablespoons freshly chopped basil

sea salt and freshly ground
  black pepper

freshly grated Parmesan and a little
  extra virgin olive oil, to serve

a 4-litre/quart Dutch oven

Serves 6

A day ahead, place the beans in a large bowl and cover with cold water. Leave to soak overnight.

The next day, drain and rinse the beans and place in the Dutch oven. Add plenty of cold water to cover the beans by at least 10 cm/4 inches. Cut 1 onion in half and add to the pan with the bay leaf. Bring the water to a rolling boil, then simmer, uncovered, for 45 minutes or until the beans are al dente. Drain the beans, reserving 1.25 litres/5 cups of the liquid but discarding the onion and bay leaf.

Finely chop the remaining onion. Heat the olive oil in the pan over a medium heat and fry the pancetta for 3–4 minutes until crisp and golden. Remove from the pan with a slotted spoon and set aside.

Add the chopped onion, carrot, potato, celery, garlic, herbs and salt and pepper to the pan and fry over a medium heat for 10 minutes until softened slightly, stirring occasionally to prevent them sticking. Add the cooked beans, passata, tomato purée, and reserved cooking liquid. Bring to the boil, then cover and simmer over a low heat for 30 minutes until the sauce is thick and rich.

Stir the pasta and reserved pancetta into the pan, return to a gentle simmer and cook for a final 10–12 minutes until the pasta is al dente. Stir in the basil and season to taste. Spoon into individual soup bowls and top each one with Parmesan and olive oil.

Another French classic, this hearty bake includes sausage (traditionally from Toulouse), cooked white beans and a duck leg confit (or duck preserved in fat). Confit is available from specialist food stores. Cassoulet was the name of the dish used to cook the stew, but a Dutch oven is equally well suited. The rich meaty stew is topped with a blanket of crispy breadcrumbs to soak up the wonderful fatty flavours. Start this recipe a day ahead.

Duck & sausage cassoulet

250 g/1½ cups dried haricot
  or cannellini beans

2 tablespoons olive oil

4 Toulouse sausages, or other quality
  pork sausages

100 g/3½ oz. smoked back bacon
  rashers/slices, cut into lardons

1 onion, finely chopped

2 garlic cloves, crushed

400-g/14-oz. can chopped tomatoes

350 ml/1½ cups chicken stock

2 sprigs of fresh rosemary

4 duck confit (see introduction)

sea salt and freshly ground
  black pepper

crisp green salad, to serve

TOPPING

3 tablespoons duck fat

150 g/2½ cups coarsely ground
  fresh white breadcrumbs

2 tablespoons freshly chopped
  flat-leaf parsley

1 garlic clove, crushed

a 5-litre/quart Dutch oven

Serves 4

A day ahead, place the beans in a bowl and cover with plenty of cold water. Leave to soak overnight.

The next day, drain the soaked beans, rinse well and place in a large saucepan. Add enough cold water to come at least 10 cm/4 inches above the beans and bring to the boil. Simmer for 45–50 minutes or until just tender. Drain well and set aside.

Preheat the oven to 170°C fan/190°C/375°F/Gas 5.

Heat the oil in the Dutch oven over a high heat. Add the sausages and fry for 5 minutes, turning often until browned. Remove from the pan and set aside.

Add the bacon and onion to the pan and fry over a medium heat for 6–8 minutes until golden. Add the garlic and fry for 2–3 minutes. Stir in the tomatoes and stock and bring to a simmer. Add the sausages, rosemary sprigs, cooked beans, duck confit and season. Bring to the boil, then transfer to the preheated oven and cook, uncovered, for 1–1½ hours, or until the beans and duck are very tender. There should be little or no stock left.

Meanwhile, make the topping. Heat the duck fat in a medium frying pan/skillet, add the breadcrumbs and stir-fry over a medium heat for 5 minutes until they are all evenly golden. Add the parsley and garlic and cook for a further 1 minute.

Remove the casserole from the oven and scatter over the crumb mixture. Let sit for 10 minutes, then serve accompanied by a crisp green salad.

East meets West in duck heaven in this delicious slow-braising recipe. The duck is braised in spices, herbs and aromatics until tender, then left to cool before it is crisped in a hot oven.

Slow-braised duck with spices, soy sauce & pears

1 onion, roughly chopped

2 leeks, trimmed and thickly sliced

4 garlic cloves, bashed

2-cm/³⁄₄-inch piece of root ginger, sliced and bashed

2 sprigs of fresh thyme, bashed

6 star anise, lightly bashed

2 cinnamon sticks, lightly bashed

1.5 kg/3¼ lb. whole duck

1 teaspoon Chinese 5 spice powder

¼ teaspoon Sichuan peppercorns, lightly bashed

1 teaspoon each sea salt and freshly ground black pepper

approx. 250 ml/1 cup chicken stock

150 g/³⁄₄ cup soft brown sugar

100 ml/¹⁄₃ cup fish sauce

3 tablespoons dark soy sauce

2 tablespoons rice wine vinegar

3 firm pears, peeled, cored and quartered

sliced spring onions/scallions and coriander/cilantro leaves, to garnish

jasmine rice, to serve

a 6-litre/quart Dutch oven

baking sheet lined with parchment paper

Serves 4

Preheat the oven to 210°C fan/230°C/450°F/Gas 8.

Place the onions, leeks, garlic, ginger, thyme and whole spices in the Dutch oven. Pierce the duck skin all over (especially the breast) with a metal skewer. Combine the Chinese 5 spice powder, Sichuan pepper and salt and rub all over the duck skin.

Place the duck on top of the vegetables and add 50 ml/3½ tablespoons water. Transfer the pan to the preheated oven and cook for 15 minutes, uncovered, rendering the fat. Then reduce the oven temperature to 120°C fan/140°C/300°F/Gas 2, cover the pan with the lid and bake for 1½–2 hours or until the meat is very tender. Transfer the duck to a board and set aside to cool for 30 minutes. Increase the oven temperature to 180°C fan/200°C/400°F/Gas 6.

Strain the remaining duck pan juices through a sieve/strainer, pressing down lightly to extract as much juice as you can. Discard the vegetables. Remove as much fat as possible from the drained liquid. Measure the juices and make up to 300 ml/1¼ cups with the chicken stock, if necessary. Set aside.

Using poultry shears or a sharp knife, cut the cooled duck in half down the breastbone and backbone. Transfer the halves, skin side up, to the prepared baking sheet, spoon some of the reserved stock over the duck halves (about 3 tablespoons will be enough), and transfer to the oven. Roast for 15 minutes, basting every 5 minutes until the duck skin is crisp and golden and the flesh heated through.

Place the remaining stock and the sugar in a saucepan and bring to a gentle simmer, stirring to dissolve the sugar. Stir in the fish sauce, soy sauce, and vinegar. Place the pears in the pan and simmer, stirring from time to time, for 10–15 minutes until the pears are tender.

Cut the duck halves into portions, place on a serving dish, add the pears and the pan juices. Scatter over some sliced spring onions and coriander leaves and serve with jasmine rice.

Obviously a Burgundy red is the ideal wine to use for this classic dish originating from its place name, but any full-bodied fruity red wine will work. Serve the casserole with creamy mashed potato. Start this recipe a day ahead.

Coq au vin

750-ml bottle red wine

1.5 kg/3¼ lb. free-range chicken

200 g/7 oz. pearl onions, peeled

2 large carrots, sliced

2 large sticks/ribs of celery, trimmed and sliced

½ teaspoon black peppercorns, lightly bruised

2 bay leaves, bashed

2 sprigs of fresh thyme, bashed

90 ml/6 tablespoons olive oil

250 g/9 oz. smoked bacon piece, rind removed and diced

250 g/9 oz. small button mushrooms, left whole or halved

1 tablespoon plain/all-purpose flour

4 tablespoons tomato purée/paste

300 ml/1¼ cups chicken stock

2 tablespoons freshly chopped flat-leaf parsley

sea salt and freshly ground black pepper

creamy mashed potato, to serve

a 4-litre/quart Dutch oven

Serves 4

A day ahead, place the wine in the Dutch oven and bring to the boil. Boil for 5 minutes until the alcohol is burnt off and the wine slightly reduced. Let this cool completely.

Cut the chicken into 8 pieces and place in a bowl. Add the onions, carrots, celery, peppercorns and herbs and pour over the cold wine. Cover the pan and put in the fridge to marinate overnight.

The next day, carefully pick out the chicken pieces, shake off any excess liquid (back into the pan) and dry the pieces on paper towels. Meanwhile, strain the marinade into a bowl and allow the vegetables to sit in the sieve/strainer to dry. Clean and dry the Dutch oven.

Preheat the oven to 140°C fan/160°C/325°F/Gas 3.

Heat half the oil in the Dutch oven over a high heat, add the diced bacon and fry for 3–4 minutes until golden. Stir in the mushrooms and season. Fry for a further 3–4 minutes until the mushrooms are golden, then remove from the pan with a slotted spoon and set aside.

Season the chicken pieces well. Heat the remaining oil in the pan until hot. Add the chicken pieces and fry in batches for 5–6 minutes, turning until browned all over. Remove to a plate and discard all but 1 tablespoon of the oil. Reduce the heat to low, add the vegetable mixture to the pan and fry for 5–6 minutes until lightly browned.

Stir the flour into the tomato purée until smooth and then add to the pan, stirring over a medium heat for 1–2 minutes until it is really thick and dry. Gradually pour in the strained marinade wine and stock, stirring constantly, until the mixture boils and thickens and you have a smooth sauce.

Return the chicken to the pan, return to the boil and cover the pan. Transfer to the preheated oven and cook for 45 minutes. Return the bacon and mushrooms to the pan, cover and cook for a further 15 minutes until the chicken is really tender. Scatter over the parsley and serve the casserole with some creamy mashed potato.

This is a lovely, deeply spiced fish curry from Sri Lanka. It uses fresh turmeric that you prepare in the same way as root ginger, by peeling and finely grating it. If you aren't able to find fresh turmeric, you can substitute 1 teaspoon ground turmeric.

Sri Lankan fish curry

750 g/1 lb. 10 oz. skinless white fish fillets, such as bream, cod or pollock

80 ml/⅓ cup tamarind juice

2 teaspoons ground cumin

2 teaspoons ground coriander

½ teaspoon chilli/chili powder

½ teaspoon sea salt

90 ml/6 tablespoons sunflower oil

2 onions, thinly sliced

a sprig of curry leaves, picked (optional)

1 cinnamon stick, lightly bashed

5 cardamom pods, lightly bashed

2 teaspoons freshly grated root ginger

4 garlic cloves, finely chopped

1-cm/½-inch piece of fresh turmeric, peeled and grated

2 medium tomatoes, finely chopped

300 ml/1¼ cups chicken, fish or vegetable stock

200 ml/¾ cup coconut milk, plus extra to serve

2 teaspoons caster/granulated sugar

freshly ground black pepper

coriander/cilantro leaves, to garnish

basmati rice, to serve

a 2–3-litre/quart Dutch oven

Serves 4

Cut the fish fillets into 2-cm/¾-inch pieces. Mix the tamarind juice, cumin, coriander, chilli powder and salt into a paste. Place 2 tablespoons of the paste in a bowl with the fish pieces and stir well to lightly coat the pieces. Set aside until ready to cook.

Heat 2 tablespoons of the oil in the Dutch oven over a medium-high heat. Add about one third of the sliced onions and stir-fry for 8–10 minutes or until crisp and golden. Transfer to paper towels to drain and set aside.

Add another 2 tablespoons of the oil to the pan, add the curry leaves, if using, cinnamon stick and cardamom pods and cook for a few seconds until fragrant. Add the ginger, garlic, turmeric and remaining onions and cook for 5–6 minutes, stirring constantly, until the onions are softened. Add the remaining paste mixture and fry for 1 minute, then stir in the tomatoes and cook for about 10 minutes until they soften and make a thick sauce. Add the stock, bring to a gentle simmer, cover and cook for 15 minutes. Stir in the coconut milk and sugar. Season to taste.

Heat the remaining oil in a large, non-stick frying pan/skillet over a high heat. Add the marinated fish in 2 batches and fry for 2–3 minutes until lightly browned. Spoon the fish and pan juices into the Dutch oven and simmer gently for 3 minutes until the fish is cooked through.

Divide between bowls and top with the crispy onions and coriander leaves. Drizzle over a little extra coconut milk if wished and serve with some basmati rice on the side.

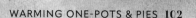

Kedgeree is a dish of spiced rice, smoked fish, aromatics, fruit and nuts that originated in India. This version of the classic dish uses whole salmon fillets, as well as the usual warming mix of spices, making it the perfect midweek supper for a cold evening.

Hot salmon kedgeree with coriander & lime

4 large skinless salmon fillets, about 180 g/6½ oz. each

8 slices of pancetta or smoked bacon rashers (rinds removed)

3 tablespoons sunflower oil

50 g/½ cup unsalted cashew nuts

1 onion, chopped

2 garlic cloves, crushed

1 teaspoon ground turmeric

½ teaspoon garam masala

300 g/1¾ cups long-grain rice

750 ml/3¼ cups chicken stock

6 whole cloves, lightly bashed

1 cinnamon stick, lightly bashed

50 g/⅓ cup raisins

1 tablespoon freshly chopped coriander/cilantro

freshly squeezed juice of 1 large lime

sea salt and freshly ground black pepper

aïoli or Greek yogurt, to serve (optional)

a 4-litre/quart Dutch oven

Serves 4

Preheat the oven to 160°C fan/180°C/350°F/Gas 4.

Wrap each salmon fillet with 2 slices of the pancetta, criss-crossing them as you go and pressing them firmly in place. Heat the oil in the Dutch oven over a medium-high heat and fry the salmon for 1 minute on each side until the pancetta is lightly golden. Remove from the pan and set aside.

Reduce the heat to medium, add the cashews to the hot oil and stir-fry for 1–2 minutes until golden, then remove with a slotted spoon and set aside.

Add the onion, garlic and some salt and pepper to the pan and fry for 6–8 minutes until the onions are softened. Stir the turmeric, garam masala and then the rice and cook over a low heat for 2 minutes. Pour in the stock, adding the cloves and cinnamon stick, and bring to a simmer. Cover the pan, transfer to the oven and bake for 30 minutes.

Remove the pan from the oven and the lid from the pan. Stir the raisins, cashew nuts, coriander and lime juice through the rice and then arrange the salmon fillets on top, pressing down gently into the rice mixture. Cover the pan, return to the oven and bake for a further 10 minutes until the salmon is cooked. Remove from the oven but let sit undisturbed for a final 5 minutes.

Divide the salmon and rice between plates and serve with some aïoli or Greek yogurt, if wished.

There is little better than a good fish pie. Here, the topping is scallop potatoes, rather than mashed potato or pastry, and it works really well. You can vary the fish if you like, but try to use some smoked fish as it adds terrific depth to the dish.

Creamy smoked fish pies with scallop potatoes

100 g/7 tablespoons butter

2 leeks, thinly sliced

3 sticks/ribs of celery, thinly sliced

40 g/¼ cup plain/all-purpose flour

350 ml/1½ cups full-fat/whole milk

150 ml/⅔ cup single/light cream

50 g/½ cup mature cheese such as Cheddar or Monterey Jack, grated

200 g/7 oz. frozen leaf spinach, thawed

250 g/9 oz. skinless salmon fillet

250 g/9 oz. smoked haddock fillet, skinned

150 g/5½ oz. cooked peeled shrimp/prawns

750 g/1 lb. 10 oz. potatoes, such as Yukon Gold, Russets, King Edwards or Desiree

sea salt and freshly ground black pepper

green beans, to serve (optional)

4 x 250-ml/9-oz individual baking dishes

Serves 4

Preheat the oven to 170°C fan/190°C/375°F/Gas 5.

Melt half the butter in a frying pan/skillet over a medium heat and fry the leeks, celery and a little salt and pepper for 10 minutes until soft but not browned. Stir in the flour and cook for a further 1 minute. Gradually add the milk and cream, stirring constantly, until the sauce is smooth. Bring to the boil, still stirring, and simmer gently for 2 minutes until thickened. Remove from the heat and stir in three-quarters of the grated cheese. Cover the entire surface with cling film/plastic wrap and set aside to cool.

Drain the spinach, squeeze out the excess water, then chop finely. Cut the salmon and smoked haddock into bite-sized pieces and cut the prawns in half. Stir the spinach, fish, prawns and a little pepper into the leek sauce, then divide equally between the individual baking dishes. Smooth flat.

Thinly slice the potatoes using either a mandolin or a very sharp knife. Melt the remaining butter and season with a little pepper. Arrange the potatoes in overlapping layers over the filling, brushing each layer with the melted butter. Finally, scatter over the remaining cheese.

Bake in the preheated oven for 30–35 minutes until the potatoes are golden and the filling bubbling. Serve with green beans, if wished.

This deliciously easy black bean stew is complemented by roasted sweet potato and a cooling yogurt and mint dressing. You can cook this either on the stovetop or in a hot oven, covered, for 30 minutes. It's a very versatile recipe so feel free to swap sweet potatoes for any squash or root vegetable and use a chicken or vegetable stock cube for extra depth.

Smoky black bean stew with sweet potatoes & minted yogurt dressing

750 g/1 lb. 10 oz. sweet potatoes

a splash of olive oil

1 tablespoon dried thyme

1 onion, diced

1 fresh red chilli/chile, deseeded and chopped

3 garlic cloves, crushed

1½ teaspoons ground cumin

1 teaspoon smoked paprika

1 teaspoon ground cinnamon

400-g/14-oz. can cherry tomatoes

2 x 400-g/14-oz. cans black beans, drained and rinsed

1 chicken or vegetable stock cube

a pinch of sugar

sea salt and freshly ground black pepper

a few sprigs of fresh coriander/ cilantro, chopped, to garnish

MINTED YOGURT DRESSING

1 garlic clove

250 g/1 cup Greek yogurt

2 tablespoons freshly chopped mint or 2 teaspoons dried mint

1 tablespoon freshly squeezed lemon juice

1½ teaspoons ground cumin

Serves 4

Preheat the oven to 200°C fan/220°C/425°F/Gas 7.

Peel and cut the sweet potatoes into irregular wedges and place on a baking sheet. Drizzle with olive oil, then season with salt, pepper and dried thyme. Bake in the preheated oven for 20–30 minutes until cooked through and slightly charred, then remove and set aside until the black bean stew is ready.

For the minted yogurt dressing, crush the garlic clove and combine with the yogurt, mint, lemon juice, a generous pinch of salt and the cumin. Set aside.

In a large pan, fry the onion in another splash of olive oil for 5 minutes until soft, then stir through the chilli and crushed garlic for a minute. Add the cumin, paprika and cinnamon, quickly followed by the tomatoes and black beans. Fill the used tomato can with cold water and pour into the pan, crumble in the stock cube and season with salt and pepper and a generous pinch of sugar. Part-cover the pan and simmer over a low heat for about 15 minutes or until the sauce has reduced and thickened. Fold the cooked sweet potatoes into the stew.

Taste for seasoning, scatter the coriander over the top and add a swirl of the minted yogurt dressing, with the rest served on the side.

This delicious bowl of goodness has just enough spice to warm your taste buds. The roasted cauliflower has a nice crunch to it so adds a bit of 'bite' to the smooth and creamy lentil dhal it is nestled on. Use red split lentils as they can be cooked from dried in ten minutes without any soaking time.

Red lentil tarka dhal with honey roasted cauliflower

ROASTED CAULIFLOWER

1 large cauliflower, broken into small florets (tender leaves cut in half)

2 tablespoons olive oil

1 tablespoon curry powder

1 tablespoon mustard seeds

a pinch of chilli/chile powder or hot smoked paprika

a pinch of salt

2 tablespoons runny honey

TARKA DHAL

200 g/1¼ cups red split lentils

15 ml/1 tablespoon olive oil

50 g/3½ tablespoons butter

1 onion, finely sliced

3 garlic cloves, chopped

5-cm/2-in. piece of fresh ginger, grated

1 teaspoon ground turmeric

½ tablespoon ground cumin

½ tablespoon cumin seeds

½ tablespoon garam masala

½ tablespoon fennel seeds

1 teaspoon salt

6 baby plum tomatoes, halved

1 green birdseye chilli/chile, chopped

TO SERVE

2 tablespoons toasted peanuts, crushed

a handful of coriander/cilantro leaves

200 g/scant 1 cup natural/plain Greek-style yogurt

4 lime wedges

Serves 4

Preheat the oven to 220°C fan/240°C/465°F/Gas 8.

Place the cauliflower florets and leaves in a large mixing bowl, pour in the olive oil and sprinkle over the curry powder, mustard seeds, chilli powder and salt. Toss to coat the florets in the oil and spices. Place them and their leaves on a large baking sheet, drizzle with the honey and pop into the oven for about 20 minutes, or until they start to crisp and brown.

While the cauliflower is cooking, make the dhal. Give the lentils a quick rinse, then put them in a saucepan with double their volume of water. Bring to the boil, then reduce to a simmer and cook uncovered for 10 minutes, skimming off any impurities as they cook. Once cooked they should have some texture but no crunch – if they are still too watery, spoon some of the liquid off. Leave to rest while you make the tarka.

To make the tarka, heat the 1 tablespoon olive oil and butter in a separate frying pan/skillet over a medium heat and sauté the onion for a few minutes until it softens. Stir in the garlic and ginger, quickly followed by all the spices and the salt. The butter will start to foam, at which point stir in the tomatoes and green chilli. Leave to cook for 1 minute, then remove from the heat.

Finally, stir a third of the tarka into the cooked lentils, then divide into serving bowls. Spoon the remaining tarka over the top of the bowls. Pile the roasted cauliflower in the centre, scatter over some peanuts and chopped coriander.

Serve with Greek yogurt for spooning and lime wedges for squeezing.

This dish is inspired by the humble food prepared in Italian villages and designed to feed a large family. Creamy polenta or mashed potato makes the perfect accompaniment for this hearty mushroom ragù. Try mixing some Parmesan through the polenta for extra depth.

Rich mushroom ragù on polenta

7 g/¼ oz. dried porcini mushrooms

olive oil, for frying/sautéing

1 medium white onion, diced

500 g/1 lb. 2 oz. chestnut or button mushrooms, halved

2 garlic cloves, sliced

1 teaspoon ground cumin

1 teaspoon smoked paprika

a small pinch of cayenne pepper

1 medium, ripe tomato, deseeded and diced

400-g/14-oz. can chickpeas, drained and rinsed

100 ml/scant ½ cup white wine

100 ml/scant ½ cup chicken or vegetable stock

a knob/pat of butter (optional)

200 g/3 cups fresh mixed wild mushrooms, cleaned

1 teaspoon freshly squeezed lemon juice

sea salt and freshly ground black pepper

creamy polenta or mashed potato, to serve

a handful of flat-leaf parsley leaves, to garnish

Serves 6

Put the dried porcini mushrooms in a heatproof measuring jug/pitcher and top up with 100 ml/scant ½ cup of just-boiled water. Leave to steep for 10 minutes, then drain (reserving the steeping liquid) and squeeze out as much moisture from the mushrooms as possible. Coarsely chop the mushrooms and set aside. Strain the steeping liquid to remove any sediment and set aside.

Set a large, heavy-based frying pan/skillet over low heat and add a splash of olive oil. Add the onion and fry for 2 minutes, then turn up the heat and add the chestnut mushrooms. Fry until golden, then stir in the soaked porcini along with the garlic, cumin, paprika and cayenne pepper.

Add the tomato, chickpeas and wine and simmer to reduce the wine until it has almost all gone. Pour the reserved mushroom steeping liquid into the pan along with the stock. Simmer until the liquid reduces by two-thirds and thickens to the consistency of single/light cream, then remove the pan from the heat. Beat in the butter, if using, and season generously with salt and pepper.

Heat a dry frying pan until smoking hot. Add a small splash of olive oil, quickly followed by the wild mushrooms and fry for 1 minute. Season with salt and pepper, add the lemon juice, then remove from the heat.

To serve, spoon the polenta or potato onto a large board or platter, making an indentation in the centre with the back of a spoon and spoon in the mushroom ragù. Scatter the wild mushrooms over the top, along with the flat-leaf parsley.

Allowing the pork to dry out in the fridge before cooking helps to crisp the skin up beautifully. The pork is then roasted in the stock, cider and milk until tender. Start this recipe up to 48 hours before cooking.

Rolled pork belly in cider with crispy crackling

2 kg/4½ lb. boneless pork belly, skin on

2 tablespoons olive oil

12 small shallots, peeled but left whole

3 large carrots, roughly chopped

3 leeks, thickly sliced

1 head of garlic, cut in half

2–3 sprigs of fresh sage

2 bay leaves, bashed

300 ml/1¼ cups hard cider

300 ml/1¼ cups chicken stock

300 ml/1¼ cups milk

sea salt and freshly ground black pepper

a 6-litre/quart Dutch oven

a baking sheet lined with parchment paper

Serves 6

At least 24 and up to 48 hours before cooking, unwrap the pork belly and place, skin side up, on a plate. Pop uncovered into the fridge to dry out thoroughly until required, remembering to remove it from the fridge 1 hour before cooking.

The day of cooking, preheat the oven to 160°C fan/180°C/350°F/Gas 4.

Using a sharp knife, carefully slice between the pork skin and the layer of fat and remove the skin in one piece (you can ask your butcher to do this for you if you prefer). Season the fat layer, then return the skin and carefully roll up the whole belly. Tie at 2-cm/¾-inch intervals with kitchen string. Rub the skin with a good sprinkling of salt and pepper.

Heat the oil in a large frying pan/skillet over a medium heat. Add the pork and cook for 8–10 minutes, turning occasionally, until the skin is golden brown and crispy. Remove from the pan.

Arrange the vegetables, garlic halves, sage sprigs and bay leaves in the Dutch oven and place the pork on top. Pour the cider, stock and milk around the pork, cover, and transfer the pan to the preheated oven. Cook for 1½ hours until the meat is tender.

Increase the oven temperature to 210°C fan/230°C/450°F/Gas 8. Remove the pan from the oven. Carefully lift the pork out onto a warm plate and snip away the string. Place the skin on the prepared baking sheet and return it to the oven for 10 minutes or so until it is really crisp.

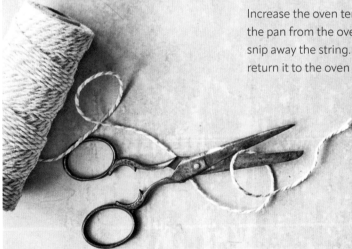

Meanwhile, using a slotted spoon, transfer the vegetables to the pork platter, cover loosely with foil and keep warm. Spoon away as much of the layer of fat from the top of the sauce as you can and bring the pan juices to the boil on the stovetop. Simmer for 3–4 minutes or until thickened.

Carve the pork into slices and the skin into strips, and serve with the vegetables and gravy.

*There is little better than chewing on a sticky,
tender and lip-smacking pork rib – only improved
by enjoying in front of a fire on a cold night perhaps.
After a long, slow braise, the ribs are returned to
the Dutch oven, brushed with the glaze and cooked
on a high heat in the oven. Perfect.*

Slow roasted pork ribs with cabbage & apple slaw

2 kg/4½ lb. pork rib racks

250 ml/1 cup hard cider

150 ml/⅔ cup pineapple juice

75 ml/¼ cup clear honey

4 tablespoons tomato purée/paste

1 teaspoon ground cinnamon

1 teaspoon smoked paprika

½ teaspoon ground allspice

1 teaspoon sea salt

fries, to serve

CABBAGE & APPLE SLAW

1 teaspoon fennel seeds

¼ green cabbage, shredded

1 small onion, very thinly sliced

1 apple, skin on, cored, quartered
and cut into thin batons

¼ teaspoon sugar

¼ teaspoon sea salt

2 teaspoon freshly squeezed
lime juice

4 tablespoons mayonnaise

an 8-litre/quart Dutch oven

Serves 4

Preheat the oven to 130°C fan/150°C/300°F/Gas 2. Line the Dutch oven with a large sheet of parchment paper so the paper comes a little way up the sides of the pan.

Cut the rib racks into 4 portions and pop them into the prepared pan. Stir the remaining ingredients together well in a jug/pitcher, then pour over the ribs. Top with a second layer of parchment paper, cover the pan with a tight fitting lid and transfer to the preheated oven. Cook for 3–4 hours, checking after 2½ hours and keeping an eye on the ribs until you see the meat starting to loosen from the bones.

Meanwhile, make the slaw. Place the fennel seeds and vegetables in a bowl. Add the sugar, salt and lime juice and stir until really well mixed. Set aside for 10 minutes. Stir in the mayonnaise and set aside.

Remove the pan from the oven and the lid from the pan. Increase the oven temperature to 210°C fan/230°C/450°F/Gas 8.

Transfer the ribs (discarding the paper) to a large platter and strain the juices into a small saucepan. Bring to the boil and simmer for 5–6 minutes until the sauce is thick and glossy.

If necessary wash the pan and dry well. Line the pan with another large sheet of parchment paper and return the ribs to the pan. Pour the sauce over the top and return to the oven. Cook for 10–15 minutes, turning and glazing halfway through until the ribs are sticky with the glaze. Allow to cool for 10 minutes, then serve the ribs with the slaw and fries.

This is an all-round winner. Tasty meatballs, a rich tomato ragù, a little cream for extra comfort, and a layer of meltingly gooey mozzarella all combine to make a type of meatball lasagne! A great midweek winter meal for the family – kids will love this one.

Oven-baked meatballs with cheesy tomato sauce

450 g/1 lb. minced/ground beef

300 g/10½ oz. minced/ground pork

1 small onion, very finely chopped

2 teaspoons English mustard

2 teaspoons freshly chopped thyme

2 tablespoons olive oil

2 x 400-g/14-oz cans chopped tomatoes

4 garlic cloves, crushed

1 teaspoon caster/granulated sugar

a pinch of dried chilli/hot red pepper flakes

4 tablespoons freshly chopped basil, plus extra to garnish

75 ml/5 tablespoons single/light cream

200 g/7 oz. mozzarella cheese, sliced

sea salt and freshly ground black pepper

pasta or bread and a crisp green salad, to serve

a 4-litre/quart Dutch oven

Serves 4–6

Combine the beef, pork, onion, mustard, thyme and plenty of salt and pepper in a bowl. Mix this together with your hands to form a really good sticky mixture. Then, using slightly damp hands, shape into 20–24 golfball-sized meatballs. Cover and let sit in a cool place for 1 hour.

Preheat the oven to 140°C fan/160°C/325°F/Gas 3.

Heat the oil in the Dutch oven, add the meatballs, and cook in batches for 3–4 minutes until evenly browned. Remove with a slotted spoon. Add the tomatoes, garlic, 1 teaspoon sea salt, sugar, dried chilli flakes and basil to the pan and bring to the boil. Pop the meatballs into the sauce, cover and transfer the pan to the preheated oven. Cook for 1 hour or until the sauce is thick and glossy and the meatballs cooked through.

Remove the pan from the oven and the lid from the pan. Very carefully pour the cream around the meatballs and then lay the mozzarella slices on top. Return to the oven, uncovered, and cook for 10–15 minutes until the cheese is melted.

Scatter with some fresh basil leaves and serve with some pasta or bread and a crisp green salad.

Turkey breast meat can be a little dry, especially when it is cooked as part of a whole bird. Here the breast only is stuffed, wrapped in prosciutto and cooked as a dish in itself. Depending on availability, you can use either 1 large turkey breast of around 1.5 kg/3¼ lb. or 2 x 750 g/1 lb. 6 oz. smaller breast fillets. Serve with this fruity festive gravy and your favourite vegetable accompaniments.

Roasted turkey breast with prosciutto & cranberry gravy

1.5 kg/3¼ lb. turkey breast fillet (or 2 smaller fillets), skinned

2 tablespoons each of freshly chopped rosemary and sage

2 garlic cloves, crushed

grated zest of 2 lemons

60 ml/4 tablespoons extra virgin olive oil

12 large slices prosciutto

25 g/1¾ tablespoons butter

CRANBERRY GRAVY

1 tablespoon plain/all-purpose flour

125 ml/½ cup white wine

250 ml/1 cup chicken stock

75 g/4 tablespoons cranberry sauce

sea salt and freshly ground black pepper

a 4-litre/quart Dutch oven

Serves 8

Preheat the oven to 180°C fan/200°C/400°F/Gas 6.

Take the turkey and, using a sharp knife, slice a pocket into the thicker side as far as you can without cutting it in half. Mix the rosemary, sage, garlic, lemon zest, 2 tablespoons of the oil and salt and pepper together and spread the mixture into the prepared pocket. Wrap the whole breast in slices of prosciutto and secure in place at 2-cm/¾-inch intervals with kitchen string.

Heat the butter and remaining oil together in the Dutch oven and sear the turkey roll for 5 minutes until golden all over. Transfer the pan to the preheated oven and roast for 40 minutes or until the juices run clear when spiked with a skewer. Remove the pan from the oven and carefully lift out the turkey roll. Wrap in a double layer of foil and rest for 10 minutes.

Meanwhile, make the gravy. Place the pan over a medium heat on the stovetop, add the flour and stir for 30 seconds until blended. Gradually whisk in the wine, stirring until the mixture comes to the boil. Simmer for 5 minutes, then stir in the chicken stock and cranberry sauce. Cook for a further 5 minutes until the sauce is thickened slightly and glossy, adjust seasoning to taste.

Pour any turkey juices collected in the foil into the gravy, then carve the breast and serve with cranberry gravy.

Note: If using smaller turkey breast fillets, you only need to cook them for about 25 minutes.

Gnocchi makes a nice change from pasta and this is an easy way to turn them into a delicious ovenbake. This cheat's recipe is a superfast mid-week winter meal, using a can of broccoli and Stilton soup to make the sauce. Serve with a tomato and red onion salad.

Oven-baked broccoli & blue cheese gnocchi

1 tablespoon olive oil

1 onion, diced

1 garlic clove, chopped

1 small head broccoli, chopped

800 g/1¾ lb. ready-made gnocchi

400-g/14-oz. can broccoli and Stilton soup

50 g/1¾ oz. cream cheese

sea salt and freshly ground black pepper

Serves 4

Preheat the oven to 200°C fan/220°C/425°F/gas 7.

Heat the olive oil in an ovenproof frying pan/skillet over a medium heat and fry the onion, garlic and broccoli for a few minutes. Add 250 ml/1 cup water, cover and leave to simmer for 6 minutes until the broccoli is cooked and tender.

Remove the lid and add the gnocchi. Pour in the soup, season generously and stir to mix everything together. Bring to a simmer and once simmering, remove from the heat, stir in the cream cheese and place the pan in the oven for 12–15 minutes, or until the gnocchi is soft and cooked.

Serve with a tomato and red onion salad on the side, if liked, and some crusty bread for mopping up the cheesy sauce.

Note: If you've got any small bits of leftover blue cheese like Stilton lurking in the fridge you can crumble that in instead of adding the cream cheese, it will just give it a stronger flavour.

Famous the world over, moussaka's layers of rich meat ragù, potato and aubergine/eggplant, topped with a white sauce, are a labour of love to create, but worth the effort. This veggie version is just as delicious and best served with a simply dressed crisp green salad.

Meatless moussaka

olive oil, for frying/sautéing

300 g/10½ oz. waxy potatoes

2 aubergines/eggplant

2 courgettes/zucchini

a few pinches of Greek dried oregano

25 g/¼ cup grated vegetarian Parmesan-style hard cheese

sea salt and freshly ground black pepper

VEGETABLE RAGÙ

1 kg/2¼ lb. mushrooms, diced

1 medium white onion, diced

2 garlic cloves, chopped

150 g/2 cups precooked brown lentils

3 tablespoons tomato purée/paste

a handful of flat-leaf parsley leaves, chopped

½ tablespoon ground cinnamon

12 grates of nutmeg

1 tablespoon Greek dried oregano

1 teaspoon soft dark brown sugar

BÉCHAMEL SAUCE

75 g/¾ stick unsalted butter

75 g/½ cup plus 1 tablespoon plain/all-purpose flour

600 ml/2½ cups whole milk

a 30 x 20-cm/12 x 8-inch ovenproof baking dish

Serves 4

Preheat the oven to 180°C fan/200°C/400°F/Gas 6.

Peel the potatoes and cut them into 5-mm/¼-inch thick slices. Cut the aubergines and zucchini into 1-cm/½-inch thick slices.

Line a tray with paper towels. Heat a splash of oil in a large frying pan/skillet set over a medium heat. Add the potato, aubergine and courgette slices in batches and fry until golden and just cooked through, then transfer to the paper towel-lined tray to drain. Arrange a layer of potato slices in the baking dish, and season with a pinch of oregano and a few grinds of black pepper. Repeat with a layer of aubergine and finally courgette, again adding oregano and seasoning between each layer.

To make the ragù, add a little oil to a medium saucepan and set over a high heat. Add the mushrooms and fry for about 15 minutes, stirring occasionally; you want these deeply caramel coloured. Turn down the heat and add the onion and cook for another 5 minutes until it has softened and coloured. Add the garlic and cook for 1 minute, then add the lentils, tomato purée, parsley, cinnamon, nutmeg, oregano and sugar. Add about 60 ml/¼ cup water and simmer, uncovered, for 10–15 minutes until the ragù is rich and thick. Spoon this over the layered vegetables, levelling the surface with the back of the spoon.

To make the béchamel sauce, melt the butter in a saucepan set over a low-medium heat. Add the flour and stir continuously until a paste forms and cook this for 2 minutes. Add the milk to the pan gradually, whisking/beating as you go, until the sauce has thickened and is smooth. Season generously with salt and pepper.

Gently pour the sauce over the ragù layer, again smoothing out the surface with the back of a spoon. Scatter the grated cheese over the top and cook in the preheated oven for 30 minutes. Leave to rest for about 15 minutes before serving with a simply dressed green salad.

Unlike risotto rice, spelt grains do not need to be stirred constantly. As the grain cooks, it does become tender but retains a lovely 'bite', adding texture to the finished dish. This makes it ideal for baking in the oven.

Baked pumpkin & spelt risotto

60 ml/4 tablespoons extra virgin olive oil

1 onion, chopped

2 garlic cloves, crushed

1 tablespoon freshly chopped rosemary, plus extra to garnish

300 g/10½ oz. spelt berries

350 g/12 oz. pumpkin flesh, grated

1 litre/4 cups vegetable stock

50 g/⅔ cup freshly grated Parmesan, plus extra to serve

50 g/¼ cup mascarpone

sea salt and freshly ground black pepper

a little butter, to serve

a 2–3-litre/quart Dutch oven

Serves 4

Preheat the oven to 160°C fan/180°C/350°F/Gas 4.

Heat the oil in the Dutch oven over a medium heat and fry the onion, garlic, rosemary, salt and pepper for 5 minutes until softened. Add the spelt berries and stir-fry for 1 minute until all the grains are glossy.

Add the pumpkin and stir well, then pour in the stock and bring to the boil. Cover the pan and transfer to the preheated oven. Bake for 45 minutes, then carefully remove the lid and check the amount of liquid left. If it is almost gone, cover and bake for a final 15 minutes, or if there is still a fair amount of the liquid, bake uncovered for a further 15 minutes. At this point the grains will be al dente.

Remove the pan from the oven and stir in the Parmesan and mascarpone. Cover and allow to sit for 5 minutes. Season to taste and serve at once dotted with a little butter, a scattering of rosemary sprigs and some extra Parmesan, if wished.

Tip: Spelt berries are readily available from either your supermarket or from health food stores; alternatively buy online.

This harvest pie is packed with canned lentils and vegetables and uses potato and leek soup to bring everything together for a hearty and savoury supper. If you were short on time, you can mix the filling directly in the pastry case and just top with a pastry lid, then into the oven for a quicker fix.

Harvest pie

500 g/1 lb. 2 oz. ready-made puff pastry

1 egg, whisked

2 x 400-g/14-oz. cans green lentils, drained and rinsed

400-g/14-oz can baby carrots and petit pois, drained and rinsed

400-g/14-oz can green beans, drained and rinsed

400-g/14-oz can potato and leek soup

25 g/3 tablespoons plain/all-purpose flour, plus extra for dusting

15 g/1 tablespoon butter, diced

1 teaspoon dried mixed herbs

1 teaspoon salt

½ teaspoon freshly ground black pepper

½ teaspoon curry powder

a 28 x 20 cm/11 x 8 inch baking pan

Serves 4

Preheat the oven to 200°C fan/220°C/425°F/Gas 7.

Cut the block of pastry in half and roll out one half on a floured work surface to about 3 mm/⅛ inch thick. Use this to line the baking pan, allowing the pastry to overhang the top lip of the pan. Line with baking parchment and baking beans (or raw rice, etc.) and blind bake in the preheated oven for 20 minutes. Remove from the oven, remove the parchment and baking beans, then brush with some of the whisked egg and return to the oven for another 5 minutes.

In a mixing bowl, gently fold all the remaining ingredients together. Pour into the baking pan on top of the cooked pastry and level out with the back of a spoon. Roll out the remaining pastry to cover the top, crimping around the edges to seal.

Pierce the top with a sharp knife to help the steam release, brush with the remaining egg and season the top. Bake in the oven for a further 30 minutes or until the top is golden. Leave to rest for at least 15 minutes to allow the filling to set before serving.

What to do with leftover turkey at Thanksgiving or Christmas? This pie is the perfect solution. Normally you would use a pie dish, but the Dutch oven works just as well for this. If you have mini dishes, you can easily make individual pies instead – cut the pastry into small circles the size of the dishes and cook for about 20 minutes.

Creamy turkey & mushroom puff pastry pie

90 ml/6 tablespoons olive oil

250 g/9 oz. button mushrooms, wiped and quartered

1 onion, finely chopped

2 leeks, trimmed and thinly sliced

2 garlic cloves, crushed

2 teaspoons freshly chopped thyme

30 g/2 tablespoons butter, softened

50 g/3½ tablespoons plain/all-purpose flour, plus extra for dusting

2 teaspoons mustard powder

500 ml/2 cups chicken stock

200 ml/¾ cup crème fraîche

400 g/14 oz. leftover cooked turkey meat, shredded

100 g/3½ oz. cooked ham, shredded or diced

2 tablespoons freshly chopped tarragon

275-g/10-oz. packet ready-made puff pastry

sea salt and freshly ground black pepper

EGG GLAZE

1 egg yolk

1 tablespoon milk

a 2–3 litre/quart Dutch oven

Serves 4–6

Heat half the oil in the Dutch oven over a high heat. Add the mushrooms and a little salt and pepper and stir-fry for 2–3 minutes until golden but not releasing their juices. Remove with a slotted spoon and set aside. Reduce the heat to medium. Add the remaining oil and fry the onion, leeks, garlic, thyme and some more salt and pepper for 6–8 minutes until really soft but not browned.

Beat the butter, flour and mustard powder together to form a paste. Stir into the pan and cook for 1 minute. Gradually stir in the stock and then the crème fraîche until you have a smooth mixture. Bring slowly to the boil, stirring constantly, until the sauce is thickened. Remove from the heat and stir in the turkey, ham, mushrooms, tarragon and salt and pepper to taste. Cover the surface with cling film/plastic wrap and let cool for 30 minutes, then discard the cling film.

Preheat the oven to 200°C fan/220°C/425°F/Gas 7.

Roll the pastry out on a lightly floured surface to about 1 cm/½ inch larger than the rim of the Dutch oven, trimming the pastry into a round (use the trimmings for decoration). Very carefully lay the pastry in the pan to completely cover the surface of the pie filling. Make a hole in the middle. Press down into the pan around the edges.

For the egg glaze, beat the yolk and milk together until smooth. Brush the pastry top with glaze (add any trimmings and glaze these, too). Bake in the preheated oven for 30–35 minutes until the pastry is puffed up, golden, and the filling bubbling below. Serve immediately.

This salmon and spinach wellington laced with spicy 'nduja (spreadable pork sausage) makes a stunning meal. 'Nduja is a useful ingredient as it keeps for ages in the fridge and goes with everything. The perfect winter warmer.

Salmon 'nduja wellington

380-g/13½-oz. can leaf spinach, drained

1 onion, diced

1 tablespoon olive oil

3 garlic cloves, chopped

a small knob/pat of butter

300 g/10½ oz. ready-made puff pastry

plain/all-purpose flour, for dusting

60 ml/4 tablespoons 'nduja (or use a jar of 'nduja pesto or sundried tomato pesto)

1 tablespoon dried oregano

60 ml/4 tablespoons tomato purée/paste

2 x 213-g/7½-oz. cans pink salmon, drained, skin and bones removed

1 egg, whisked

TO SERVE

300-g/10½-oz. can broad/fava beans

400-g/14-oz. can baby carrots and petit pois

a knob/pat of butter

2 sprigs of fresh mint

hollandaise sauce or gravy

sea salt and freshly ground black pepper

Serves 4

Preheat the oven to 200°C fan/220°C/425°F/Gas 7.

Place the spinach in a sieve/strainer, pushing it down with the back of a spoon to squeeze out as much liquid as possible.

Fry the onion in the olive oil for a few minutes to soften and caramelize, then add the garlic and cook for another minute. Add the spinach and fry for a few more minutes until all the moisture has evaporated. Remove from the heat and fold in the butter, then spread the spinach onto a plate to cool down.

Roll out the pastry on a work surface dusted with flour to approximately 45 x 20 cm/18 x 8 inches and place on a piece of baking parchment. Mix the 'nduja, oregano and tomato purée together and spread over the pastry with the back of a spoon, leaving a border of 2.5 cm/1 inch at the two short ends of the pastry. Spread the spinach over the top of the tomato mixture using the back of a fork to even it out.

Taking a small handful of salmon at a time, give it a very gentle squeeze to remove a little of the moisture and form a line of salmon the length of the pastry on one side (leave a gap of 2.5 cm/1 inch at both ends). Lift the parchment and roll the pastry over the salmon filling to make a tightly enclosed log. Pinch the ends together to seal and brush with egg. Make a few small slits in the top to let steam escape and season with a pinch of salt. Slide onto a large baking sheet. Bake in the preheated oven for 20–25 minutes or until golden.

Tip both cans of vegetables into a pan, heat until piping hot, then drain, stir through the butter and season well. Just before serving, garnish with mint leaves. Use a bread knife to carve the salmon wellington. Some say you should serve it with hollandaise sauce, but instant gravy works just as well.

Winter salads

Radicchio has a striking red and white colour and natural bitterness that, when roasted, mellows to a warm smokiness. A tangy blue cheese dressing with crunchy walnuts and seeds is all it needs, oh and a little drizzle of sticky pomegranate molasses...

Roasted radicchio with blue cheese dressing

100 g/½ cup pearled spelt

2 medium radicchio heads

a splash of olive oil

2 tablespoons butter, melted

1 tablespoon runny honey

4 walnuts halves, crumbled

1 tablespoon toasted pumpkin seeds/pepitas

2 tablespoons pomegranate molasses

sea salt and freshly ground black pepper

BLUE CHEESE DRESSING

50 g/2 oz. any blue cheese

3 tablespoons Greek yogurt

2 tablespoons extra virgin olive oil

a few squeezes of fresh lemon juice

a pinch of finely chopped flat-leaf parsley

a pinch of salt

Serves 4–6

Preheat the oven to 200°C fan/220°C/425°F/Gas 7.

Rinse the pearled spelt under running water. Tip into a large saucepan and cover with salted water. Simmer for about 20–30 minutes, or until cooked; it should be chewy but without any crunch. Drain, season and set aside.

Trim the radicchio and quarter lengthways (or cut into sixths if they are on the large side) and put them on a baking sheet. Drizzle with a little olive oil, the melted butter and just a smidge of honey and season with salt and pepper. Toss with your hands to coat evenly. Roast in the preheated oven for about 15–20 minutes, turning them once during cooking. They are done when the stalk is just knife tender. Pour the cooked spelt into the baking sheet to coat in any of the juices, then transfer everything to a serving dish or platter.

To make the Blue Cheese Dressing, simply mash all the ingredients together with a fork in a small bowl and add a splash of water if it needs loosening to a pouring consistency. Drizzle the dressing over the radicchio and spelt, sprinkle with crumbled walnuts and pumpkin seeds and finish with a drizzle with pomegranate molasses.

Here's a classic combination of ingredients. Amaranth provides a base which is neither sweet nor savoury, but which has a subtle, slightly peppery taste, while the delicate poached trout ramps up the nutritional value. It looks great served on a larger platter to share or plate up individual servings, and it's gluten-free too.

Poached trout, shaved carrot, corn & amaranth with a mustard & dill dressing

4 trout fillets, skin removed

1 lemon, thickly sliced

1 tablespoon white wine vinegar

2 tablespoons olive oil

3 corn cobs, kernels removed

200 g/2 cups amaranth, cooked according to package instructions

2 carrots, julienned on a mandoline

2 tablespoons capers

1 red onion, thinly sliced

sea salt and freshly ground black pepper

chickpea tops or other mini herbs, to garnish

MUSTARD DILL DRESSING

1 tablespoon wholegrain mustard

1 teaspoon Dijon/French mustard

2 teaspoons caster/superfine sugar

6 tablespoons olive oil

2 tablespoons freshly squeezed lemon juice, or to taste

2 tablespoons finely chopped dill

2 teaspoons jarred horseradish, or to taste

Serves 4–6

Start by placing the trout fillets in a large, high-sided pan with the sliced lemon and white wine vinegar. Cover with cold water, place over a low heat and bring to a simmer. Poach for about 10 minutes, until the fish is just cooked through. Remove from the pan, allow to cool a little, then flake into large chunks.

For the dressing, whisk the mustards and sugar in a bowl to combine, then gradually add the olive oil in a thin steady stream, whisking until thick and emulsified. Whisk in the remaining ingredients and season to taste.

Meanwhile, heat a frying pan/skillet over a high heat, add 1 tablespoon olive oil, then add the corn kernels and season well. Cook for 5–6 minutes until the corn is charred and crispy. Place on a serving platter with the cooked amaranth.

Top with the remaining olive oil and season well. Add the carrots, capers, red onion and chickpea tops or herbs, then the poached trout. Serve with the mustard dill dressing drizzled over.

Halloumi, like feta, is traditionally made with a mixture of sheep's and goat's milk and is a similarly salty, sweet yet slightly sharp cheese. Unlike feta however, halloumi is never eaten raw, it is always melted and is a dish in its own right. Here it is paired with a Middle Eastern salad called fattoush, a combination of finely chopped salad vegetables, griddled flatbreads and loads of freshly chopped herbs, all seasoned with lemon juice and olive oil. A creamy tahini sauce offsets the sharpness of the cheese and salad.

Halloumi & fattoush salad with crispy flatbreads

2 large flatbreads

1 large green (bell) pepper, deseeded and diced

1 cucumber (ideally Lebanese), diced

2 ripe tomatoes, diced

1 small red onion, finely chopped

2 tablespoons freshly chopped parsley

2 tablespoons freshly chopped coriander/cilantro

3 tablespoons extra virgin olive oil

1 tablespoon freshly squeezed lemon juice

250 g/9 oz. halloumi, drained and cut into 8 slices

a handful of rocket/arugula leaves

TAHINI SAUCE

200 g/¾ cup Greek yogurt

2 tablespoons tahini paste

1 small garlic clove, crushed

1 tablespoon freshly squeezed lemon juice

salt and freshly ground black pepper

a pinch of dukkah, for sprinkling

a raclette or grill/broiler

Serves 4

Heat a large griddle pan or frying pan/skillet until hot and cook the flatbreads for 1 minute on each side until lightly charred. Leave to cool and crisp up, then tear into bite-sized pieces. Set aside.

Mix together the green pepper, cucumber, tomatoes, onion and herbs in a bowl. Add the flatbread pieces and stir in the olive oil and lemon juice. Season to taste.

To make the tahini sauce, combine all the ingredients in a bowl.

Heat the raclette machine or a conventional grill/broiler to the highest setting. Place the halloumi slices on the raclette trays and cook for 2–3 minutes until softened and bubbling (they probably won't brown).

Meanwhile, invite your guests to help themselves to the tahini sauce, fattoush and rocket leaves. As soon as the cheese is melted, scrape or spoon it directly on to the fattoush on everyone's plates and scatter over a pinch of dukkah.

This is a lovely winter warmer salad. Dolcelatte, meaning 'sweet milk', is an Italian cow's milk blue cheese with a soft, creamy texture and mild taste. It is a vegetarian cheese made without animal rennet and is often described as a milder version of Gorgonzola. It is perfect for this recipe, but you could use other mild blue cheeses such as Cambozola or a young Gorgonzola.

Dolcelatte & sweet potato salad with caramelized pecans

750 g/1 lb. 10 oz. sweet potatoes

1 large red onion, cut into thin wedges

2 tablespoons extra virgin olive oil

100 g/3½ oz. pecan nuts

3 tablespoons maple syrup

½ teaspoon smoked paprika

¼ teaspoon cayenne pepper

¼ teaspoon sea salt

200 g/7 oz. green beans, trimmed and halved

100 g/3 oz. baby spinach leaves

200 g/7 oz. Dolcelatte or other good melting blue cheese

sea salt and freshly ground black pepper

crusty bread, to serve

DRESSING

3 tablespoons freshly squeezed orange juice

2 teaspoons sherry vinegar

½ teaspoon caster/granulated sugar

3 tablespoons extra virgin olive oil

1 tablespoon walnut oil

a large roasting pan lined with parchment paper

a raclette or grill/broiler

Serves 4–6

Preheat the oven to 180°C fan/200°C/400°F/Gas 6.

Cut the sweet potatoes into 2-cm/¾-inch chunks and place in the prepared pan with the onion wedges. Add the oil and some salt and pepper, then stir well to make sure the chunks of sweet potato are evenly coated. Roast in the preheated oven for 40–50 minutes until the potatoes are caramelized and the onion browned. Remove from the oven and cool until just warm.

Meanwhile, place the pecans in a heavy non-stick frying pan/skillet and put over a medium heat. Add the maple syrup, paprika, cayenne pepper and salt. Heat gently until it starts to bubble, then cook for 3 minutes until golden and sticky. Transfer the pecans to a piece of baking paper and let cool. Separate them if stuck together and chop roughly.

Cook the green beans in a saucepan of lightly salted, boiling water for 2 minutes. Drain and refresh under cold water. Drain well and pat dry.

To make the dressing, whisk together all the ingredients in a small bowl and season to taste. Put the spinach leaves in a large bowl and add the roasted sweet potato mixture, caramelized pecans and beans.

Heat the raclette machine or a conventional grill/broiler to the highest setting. Divide the cheese between the individual raclette trays and cook for 2–3 minutes until softened and bubbling. Dress the salad and divide between plates. Pour or scrape the cheese over the salad and serve with crusty bread.

Rounds of creamy white goat's cheese are melted under a raclette grill and served on a bruschetta with roasted baby beetroot/beets, salad leaves and toasted walnuts – a classic combination. If you can, serve the finished dish drizzled with a good-quality walnut oil. If you aren't able to find Rocamadour, use a log of goat's cheese, cut into 1-cm/½-inch thick slices.

Goat's cheese bruschetta with roasted beetroot

500 g/1 lb. 2 oz. baby beetroot/ beets

1 tablespoon olive oil

4 slices of ciabatta

1 garlic clove, peeled but left whole

50 g/2 oz. walnuts, toasted and roughly chopped

a handful each of rocket/arugula or mixed salad leaves

200 g/7 oz. Rocamadour or a goat's cheese log, sliced

sea salt and freshly ground black pepper

walnut or extra virgin olive oil and reduced balsamic vinegar (see note below), to serve

a small roasting pan lined with parchment paper

a raclette or grill/broiler

Serves 4

Preheat the oven to 160°C fan/180°C/350°F/Gas 4.

Wash and dry the beetroot (reserving any small tender leaves for the salad) and place in the prepared pan. Drizzle with the olive oil and season with salt and pepper. Cover the pan with foil and bake in the preheated oven for 40–45 minutes (depending on size) until tender. Once cooked, transfer to a bowl, cover with the foil and set aside to cool. Cut into halves or slices, discarding the skin.

Chargrill the ciabatta and rub all over with garlic. Place a slice of ciabatta on each serving plate and top with the beetroot, walnuts, rocket leaves, walnut or olive oil, reduced balsamic vinegar and some salt and pepper.

Just before serving, heat the raclette machine or a conventional grill/ broiler to its highest setting. Divide the cheese slices between the raclette trays and cook for 2–3 minutes until completely melted. As soon as the cheese is ready, slide it over the bruschetta and serve.

Note: To make your own reduced balsamic vinegar, simply boil a 750-ml/3-cup bottle of inexpensive balsamic vinegar in a small saucepan for 6–8 minutes until it is reduced and syrup-like. Cool and store in a sterilized bottle. It will keep until used up.

This is simple to make and such a satisfying dish to eat on colder days. Butternut squash contrasts nicely with the dark and earthy lentils and if you've got some feta lurking in the fridge, throw a few crumbs on top to serve.

Roast squash & lentil salad

1 x 1-kg/2 lb. 4-oz. winter squash, such as butternut, pumpkin, hubbard or acorn

about 4 tablespoons olive oil

a couple of pinches of dried oregano

a few sprigs of fresh rosemary

6 garlic cloves, unpeeled and halved

1 x 250-g/9-oz. packet of cooked Puy lentils

1 x 250-g/9-oz. packet of cooked green lentils

½ red onion, thinly sliced

100 g/3½ oz. cooked beetroot/beet, cut into wedges

a small handful freshly chopped flat-leaf parsley

2 tablespoons red wine vinegar

sea salt and freshly ground black pepper

Serves 8 to share, 4 as a main

Preheat the oven to 180°C fan/200°C/400°F/Gas 6.

Peel and deseed the squash and cut the flesh into 2.5-cm/1-inch slices (if you are using butternut, you can leave the skin on as it will cook okay). Put the squash pieces in a bowl and add a glug of olive oil, the oregano, rosemary and garlic, then mix well.

Tip into a roasting pan and roast in the preheated oven for 30 minutes, or until the squash is tender and cooked and starting to brown at the edges.

Tip both the Puy and green lentils into a large bowl and add the red onion, beetroot wedges and chopped parsley. Dress the salad with a generous amount of the remaining olive oil and a splash of red wine vinegar – taste and adjust the balance of olive oil and vinegar to taste. Season with salt and pepper.

To serve, add the roasted squash to the bowl and fold it into the lentils, along with any cooking juices in the pan.

Desserts & sweet bakes

Inspired by a dessert at the Ivy restaurant in central London, this dessert of frozen summer berries is warmed with a hot white chocolate sauce poured over it immediately before serving. The warmth of the sauce caresses the berries and softens them, while retaining a delightful cool crispness. This version has the added delight of meringue kisses for extra crunch.

Frozen summer berries with white chocolate custard

300 ml/1¼ cups full-fat/whole milk

250 ml/1 cup double/heavy cream

1 vanilla pod/bean, split

5 egg yolks

2 tablespoons caster/granulated sugar

2 teaspoons cornflour/cornstarch

150 g/5½ oz. white chocolate, chopped

500 g/1 lb. 2 oz. mixed frozen summer berries

MERINGUE KISSES

2 egg whites

60 g/5 tablespoons caster/granulated sugar

a pinch of salt

a few drops of vanilla extract

a baking sheet lined with parchment paper

a fondue pot and tabletop burner (optional)

Serves 4

First make the meringue kisses. Preheat the oven to 100°C fan/120°C/250°F/Gas ½.

Whisk the egg whites in a bowl until foamy, then add the sugar a spoonful at a time and mix until the mixture is thickened and glossy. Finally, whisk in the salt and vanilla extract. Spoon or pipe small 2-cm/¾-inch rounds of meringue onto the prepared baking sheet and bake in the preheated oven for 35–40 minutes until the kisses are set. Remove from the oven and cool on the trays. Store in an airtight container.

Make the sauce. Heat the milk, cream and vanilla pod together in a pan set over a gentle heat until it reaches boiling point, then remove from the heat and set aside to infuse for 20 minutes. Discard the vanilla pod.

Whisk the egg yolks, sugar and cornflour together in a bowl until pale and creamy, then stir in the infused milk. Pour the custard into your fondue pot and on the stovetop, heat gently, stirring constantly, until the mixture thickens to coat the back of the spoon. Remove the pan from the heat and gradually stir in the chocolate until melted. Transfer the fondue pot to the tabletop burner.

Remove the berries from the freezer and spoon into bowls or glasses. Diners can now ladle the hot sauce directly from the pot on to the frozen berries, allowing them to melt and soften just a little. Serve with the meringue kisses.

Tip: If you don't have a fondue pot and tabletop burner, you can just make the sauce in the saucepan and transfer to a jug/pitcher for pouring over the berries at the table.

This recipe works perfectly for a fancy winter dinner party or just as an indulgent weekend dessert. If you want a non-alcoholic version for all the family, substitute grape juice for the red wine.

Poached pears with orange blossom chantilly cream

4 conference pears

750-ml/3-cup bottle of red wine or red grape juice

200 g/1 cup caster/granulated white sugar

5-cm/2-in. cinamon stick

12 black peppercorns

1 orange

a few mint leaves, to garnish

Orange Blossom Chantilly Cream, to serve (see below)

ORANGE BLOSSOM CHANTILLY CREAM

300 ml/1¼ cups double/heavy cream

2 tablespoons icing/confectioners' sugar

a few drops of vanilla extract

½ teaspoon orange blossom extract

Serves 4

Peel the pears leaving the stalk intact, then trim the base with a paring knife so they stand upright.

Pour the wine or grape juice into a tight-fitting saucepan and add the sugar, cinnamon, peppercorns and a 7.5-cm/3-inch piece of orange rind, plus a little squeeze of the orange juice (about 1 tablespoon, give or take). Warm the liquid over medium heat, stirring, until the sugar is dissolved, then carefully place the pears into the saucepan – it's okay if they fall over.

Bring to a simmer and poach for 45 minutes, or until the pears are soft with only a little resistance when a knife is inserted. Once cooked, remove the pears from the saucepan (I find a wooden spoon is best to avoid damaging the pears) and leave to cool.

Meanwhile, return the pan to the heat and simmer until the sauce is reduced by half and nice and glossy. You can at this stage pop everything into the fridge and reheat when you want to serve.

Whisk the cream with the icing sugar, vanilla extract and orange blossom extract until you have soft, billowy peaks; don't over-whisk the cream. Taste, adding more orange blossom extract if needed, then cover and chill in the fridge until ready to serve.

To serve, stand a pear proud in a serving bowl. Pour the sauce over the pear to make it glossy, it will pool in the bowl too. If you want to be fancy you can cut a small insertion at the top of the pear and push a mint leaf in, otherwise just scatter a few into each bowl. Serve with a dollop of the orange blossom chantilly cream on the side.

Note: If you made this in advance, reheat the pears in the microwave for a minute; just to warm and take the chill off and heat the sauce in a saucepan to warm through.

Pedro Ximénez is a divine sweet sherry from Jerez in Spain's sherry-producing region. It is raisin-y, with chocolatey notes that blends beautifully with both the peaches and the melted cheese. You could substitute either Madeira or Marsala for the sherry, although Pedro Ximénez is best. This is a wonderfully soothing and warming dessert, perfect for a cold winters night.

Peaches with raclette & cinnamon

50 g/3½ tablespoons unsalted butter

50 g/¼ cup soft brown sugar

½ teaspoon ground cinnamon

4 fresh peaches, halved and stoned

100 ml/7 tablespoons Pedro Ximénez, Madeira or Marsala

50 ml/3½ tablespoons double/ heavy cream, plus extra to serve

4 thick slices brioche loaf

4 slices raclette cheese, or 100 g/3½ oz. raclette, thinly sliced

2 tablespoons flaked/slivered almonds, toasted

a raclette or grill/broiler

Serves 4

Heat the butter, sugar and cinnamon together in a heavy frying pan/ skillet. When bubbling, add the peach halves, cut side down and cook over a high heat for 2–3 minutes until lightly golden. Remove the peaches with a slotted spoon to a foil-lined tray. Return the frying pan to the heat and stir in the Pedro Ximénez and cream. Simmer for 5 minutes until you have a thickened, caramel sauce. Keep warm.

Heat the raclette machine or a conventional grill/broiler to its highest setting so the top plate is hot. Place the pan of peaches on the heat to keep warm.

Meanwhile, toast the brioche slices either under the raclette grill or a conventional grill/broiler and arrange on warm serving plates.

Lay the Raclette slices on the individual raclette trays and grill/broil for 3–4 minutes until bubbling and melted. Carefully spoon 2 peach halves onto each slice of brioche and slide the melted cheese over the top. Immediately drizzle with the warm caramel sauce, a little more cream and serve scattered with the toasted almonds.

Orange & Cardamom Fondue

1 tablespoon green cardamom pods

very finely grated zest of 1 large orange , plus 125 ml/½ cup freshly squeezed juice

2 egg yolks

1 egg

60 g/5 tablespoons caster/ granulated sugar

CARAMEL GRAPES & DATES

250 g/9 oz. grapes

125 g/4½ oz. fresh or semi-dried dates

225 g/1 cup plus 2 tablespoons caster/ granulated sugar

a fondue pot and tabletop burner (optional)

Serves 4

Divide the grapes into small bunches and spear each date with a bamboo skewer. Put the sugar into a heavy-based saucepan, add 60 ml/ 4 tablespoons water and heat, stirring until the sugar has dissolved. Bring to the boil but do not stir – you can gently swirl the pan around so the sugar colours evenly. Boil for 5 minutes until the sugar is a golden caramel. Remove from the heat and, working quickly, dip bunches of grapes and dates into the caramel. Put onto a plate lined with baking paper, leave for the caramel to set, then transfer to small plates.

To prepare the fondue, put the cardamom into a dry frying pan/skillet and heat for 3 minutes until aromatic. Lightly crush the pods with a mortar and pestle. Put into a small saucepan, add the orange juice and zest and simmer gently for 2 minutes. Remove from the heat, let cool, then strain and measure 60 ml/¼ cup.

Put the egg yolks, egg and sugar into a heatproof bowl set over simmering water. Using electric beaters, whisk the mixture for 10 minutes until thick and mousse-like. Gradually whisk in the measured orange and cardamom mixture and continue whisking for 5 minutes. Pour into a fondue pot and set over its tabletop burner, or into individual glasses, then serve with the dates and grapes.

Homemade doughnuts are easy to make and wonderfully light, fluffy and far less oily than shop-bought ones. It is best to eat these as hot as you can after cooking, so work your timings back from serving and it should be no problem at all. Enjoy by the fire for a cosy evening treat.

Doughnuts with salted bourbon caramel

2 teaspoons dried active yeast

125 ml/½ cup warmed milk

2 tablespoons caster/granulated sugar, plus extra for dusting

375 g/2⅔ cups unbleached white bread flour, plus extra for dusting

1 teaspoon vanilla extract

15 g/1 tablespoon unsalted butter, melted

2 medium eggs, beaten

sunflower or vegetable oil, for frying

SALTED BOURBON CARAMEL SAUCE

250 g/9 oz. milk chocolate, chopped

60 g/4 tablespoons unsalted butter

60 g/5 tablespoons light muscovado sugar

60 ml/4 tablespoons double/ heavy cream

1 tablespoon bourbon or whisky

a pinch of sea salt

10-cm/4-inch doughnut ring or round cookie cutter

a fondue pot and tabletop burner (optional)

Serves 8

To make the doughnuts, place the yeast and warm milk in a bowl with a pinch of the sugar and 1 tablespoon flour. Stir well to dissolve the yeast and set aside to froth for 10 minutes. Sift the remaining flour into a large bowl and make a well in the middle. Add the frothed yeast mixture, vanilla extract, melted butter and egg and work the mixture together with your hands to form a fairly sticky dough. Cover the bowl with cling film/plastic wrap and rest for 15 minutes.

Knead the dough on a well-floured surface for 5 minutes until smooth. Shape it into a ball and place in a lightly oiled bowl. Cover and leave to rise for 1 hour or until doubled in size.

Very gently, remove the risen dough from the bowl and using your fingers, press to form a 1.5-cm/⅝-inch thick rectangle. Using the doughnut ring or cookie cutter, stamp out as many doughnuts as you can. (You can re-roll the dough to stamp out more, but I prefer to simply fry the odds and ends left over from the doughnut rings.)

To make the sauce, place the chocolate, butter and sugar in a fondue pot, if using, or saucepan and heat gently on the stovetop, stirring constantly, until melted. Whisk in the cream and cook for 2–3 minutes until the sauce has thickened. Remove from the heat and allow the bubbles to subside, then stir in the bourbon and salt. Transfer the fondue pot to the tabletop burner on a low setting to keep warm.

Heat 5 cm/2 inches of oil in a heavy saucepan until it reaches 180°C/350°F. Fry the doughnuts in two batches for 3 minutes, turning halfway through, until they are puffed up and golden. Drain immediately on paper towels, dust with sugar if you wish and keep warm in the oven.

Arrange the doughnuts on a plate for diners to spear and dunk into the salted bourbon caramel sauce (any leftover sauce will keep in the fridge for a week).

A Dutch oven is the ideal pan in which to steam a sponge pudding. The water in the base of the pan will happily simmer away while the pudding, in its own basin, cooks to perfection.

Pumpkin, fig & maple syrup steamed pudding

softened butter, for greasing

125 g/³/₄ cup dried figs, chopped

75 g/¹/₂ cup dried dates, stoned and chopped

50 g/scant ¹/₂ cup sultanas/golden raisins

250 ml/1 cup boiling black tea, freshly made

1 teaspoon baking powder

¹/₂ teaspoon baking soda/ bicarbonate of soda

75 g/¹/₃ cup butter, softened

75 g/6 tablespoons soft brown sugar

2 eggs, lightly beaten

200 g/1¹/₂ cups self-raising/rising flour

1 teaspoon ground mixed spice

200 g/7 oz. peeled pumpkin, finely grated (about 550 g/ 1 lb. 4 oz. before peeling)

75 g/4 tablespoons maple syrup or golden syrup, plus extra to serve

vanilla custard, cream or ice cream, to serve

a 1.5-litre/6-cup pudding basin

a small trivet or baking ring

an 8-litre/quart Dutch oven

Serves 6

Grease a the pudding basin generously with the softened butter. Cut a circle of parchment paper about 5 cm/2 inches larger than the pudding basin and cut 2 sheets of foil, again about 5 cm/2 inches larger than the basin. Make a pleat along the middle of the paper, then do the same with the double layer of foil.

Place the dried fruits in a bowl and add the boiling tea, baking powder, and/bicarbonate of soda. Stir well and set aside for 15 minutes to froth.

Beat the butter and sugar together until pale and creamy, then gradually beat in the eggs a little at a time until smooth. Fold in the flour and mixed spice until combined (it will be quite dry at this stage), then stir the pumpkin and dried fruit mixture and the soaking liquid into the bowl until evenly blended.

Spoon the maple syrup into the base of the prepared pudding basin and carefully spoon in the sponge mixture, covering the syrup layer. Top with the pleated parchment paper, then the double layer of pleated foil and tie this tightly in place with kitchen string, making sure you have a piece long enough to go twice around the basin and leave enough to make a handle.

Place the trivet (or a baking ring) in the base of the Dutch oven and place the pudding basin on top of the trivet. Carefully pour in enough boiling water to come two-thirds of the way up the side of the basin. Place over a high heat and bring the water back to the boil. Reduce the heat to very low, cover the pan, and steam for 2¹/₂–3 hours. Check after 2¹/₂ hours – press a skewer into the pudding, through the foil and the paper right down to the base. Leave it there briefly, then pull it out. It should be clean and very hot to the touch (don't burn yourself) to be sure it is cooked.

Once cooked, carefully remove the basin from the pan and set aside for 10 minutes. Remove the string, foil, and paper and invert the pudding onto a serving plate. Drizzle over some extra syrup. Serve in wedges with homemade vanilla custard, cream or ice cream.

This versatile dish can be easily adapted to any time of year, using pretty much any fruit you like. For example, stick with these colder weather fruits for a winter warmer dessert, or use berries and stone fruit, peaches and raspberries or cherries and apricots in the summer.

Baked orchard fruit cobbler with cinnamon crème fraîche

8 large plums

3 pears

250 g/2 cups fresh blackberries

1 tablespoon crème de cassis (optional)

4 tablespoons soft brown sugar

COBBLER TOPPING

180 g/1⅓ cups plain/all-purpose flour

1½ teaspoons baking powder

a pinch of salt

75 g/⅓ cup unsalted butter, diced

50 g/¼ cup granulated/caster sugar

125–150 ml/½–⅔ cup buttermilk

CINNAMON CRÈME FRAÎCHE

150 g/¾ cup crème fraîche

2 teaspoons icing/confectioner's sugar, sifted

a little ground cinnamon

a 2-litre/quart Dutch oven

Serves 6

Preheat the oven to 170°C fan/190°C/375°F/Gas 5.

Halve, stone and thickly slice the plums. Peel, core and thinly slice the pears. Wash and dry the blackberries. Place the fruit in a bowl, add the cassis, if using, and brown sugar, and stir well to combine. Transfer the fruit to the Dutch oven.

To make the topping, sift the flour, baking powder and salt into a bowl and rub in the butter to make fine crumbs. Stir in the sugar. Work in enough buttermilk to bring the mixture together to make a slightly sticky dough. Spoon mounds of the topping over the fruit layer, allowing some fruit to remain uncovered.

Transfer the Dutch oven to the preheated oven and bake uncovered for about 30–35 minutes until the topping is risen and golden and the fruit is oozing rich juices. Check halfway through and cover the pan with the lid if the top is beginning to over-brown.

Meanwhile, make the cinnamon crème fraîche. Stir the crème fraîche, sugar and cinnamon together until combined. Serve with the fruit cobbler.

A Dutch oven provides a great alternative to a regular cake pan for this classic upside-down cake. The cast iron maintains an even temperature so the cake can be cooked at a slightly lower heat than if using a regular cake pan.

Upside-down pineapple & coconut cake with rum cream

½ ripe pineapple
  (about 600 g/1 lb. 4 oz.)

a little toasted coconut, to decorate

SAUCE

125 g/½ cup plus 1 tablespoon butter

125 g/scant ⅔ cup soft brown sugar

a pinch of salt

1 tablespoon pineapple juice

SPONGE

150 g/⅔ cup unsalted butter, softened,
  plus extra for greasing

200 g/1 cup caster/granulated sugar

a pinch of salt

3 large eggs, lightly beaten

200 g/1½ cups self-raising/rising
  flour, sifted

75 g/1 cup desiccated/shredded
  coconut

½ teaspoon baking powder

125 ml/½ cup sour cream
  or crème fraîche

RUM CREAM

100 g/½ cup mascarpone

50 ml/3½ tablespoons heavy/
  double cream

2 tablespoons icing/confectioner's
  sugar

1 tablespoon golden rum

*a round 2-litre/quart Dutch oven
  (or 24-cm/9½-inch width)*

Serves 8–10

Preheat the oven to 140°C fan/160°C/325°F/Gas 3. Rub the softened butter over the insides of the Dutch oven.

Peel the pineapple and cut it into 1-cm/½-inch thick slices – you will need 5 slices to cover the base of the pan. Using a small cookie cutter, stamp out and discard the central core. Use the remaining pineapple half to squeeze out the juice – you only need 1 tablespoon.

To make the sauce, put the butter, soft brown sugar, salt and the pineapple juice into a small saucepan and place over a medium heat. Cook, stirring, until the butter is melted and sugar dissolved. Bring to a simmer and cook for 2 minutes until it starts to thicken. Carefully pour the mixture into the greased pan and set aside to cool for 20 minutes, then arrange the pineapple slices in the cooled sauce.

Place all the sponge ingredients in a food processor and blend until smooth. Carefully spoon the mixture over the sauce and pineapple slices, spreading it smooth. Cover the pan with its lid, transfer to the preheated oven and bake for 40–45 minutes until the cake is risen and firm to the touch. Insert a metal skewer into the centre of the cake and remove. The skewer should be clean, if so the cake is cooked; if it is sticky, return to the oven and cook for a further 5–10 minutes.

Remove the pan from the oven, remove the lid, and let it sit for 10 minutes. Place a large plate upside down over the top of the Dutch oven and using oven mitts (or a thick tea/dish towel) very carefully invert the pan to unmould the cake. Leave to cool.

To make the rum cream, place all the ingredients in a bowl and, using an electric mixer, beat together until thickened. Cut the cake into wedges and serve with the rum cream and some toasted coconut.

Tip: It is not necessary to line the pan with parchment paper, but oil the sides of the pan to help prevent the sponge layer from sticking.

Here's a great way to adapt a classic bonfire treat into a more formal dining experience. Speculoos biscuits (those little spiced cookies so often served in Europe with a cup of coffee) make a perfect dipper for this marshmallow-topped chocolate fondue.

Malted milk s'mores

325 g/11½ oz. milk chocolate, chopped
150 ml/⅔ cup single/light cream
1½ tablespoons malted milk powder
100 g/3½ oz. small marshmallows

SPECULOOS BISCUITS

300 g/2¼ cups plain/all-purpose flour
1 tablespoon ground mixed spice
1 teaspoon ground ginger
½ teaspoon baking powder
¼ teaspoon ground cinnamon
a pinch of freshly ground black pepper
100 g/7 tablespoons butter, diced
225 g/1 cup plus 2 tablespoons
    soft brown sugar
1 small egg, beaten
*2 large baking sheets lined with
    parchment paper*
fondue pan (optional)
*raclette trays or individual gratin dishes
    (12 cm/5 inches in diameter)*

Serves 4

To make the biscuits/cookies, sift the flour, spices and pepper into a bowl until combined. Rub the butter into flour until the mixture resembles fine crumbs. Stir in the sugar and then gradually work in the egg and 2–3 teaspoons water to form a soft dough. Knead lightly into a ball, wrap in cling film/plastic wrap and refrigerate for 30 minutes.

Preheat the oven to 150°C fan/170°C/325°F/Gas 3.

Remove the dough from the fridge and roll on a lightly floured surface to form a log about 20 cm/8 inches long and 5 cm/2 inches in diameter. Start shaping the log into a flatter rectangle using a rolling pin and parchment paper until it is about 3 cm/1¼ inches in height. Using a sharp knife, cut each piece of dough into 2-mm/⅛-inch thick biscuits and arrange on the prepared baking sheets leaving a 3-cm/1¼-inch gap between each one. Bake in the preheated oven for 15 minutes until lightly golden. Remove from the oven and transfer to a wire tray to cool completely. Store in an airtight container until required.

To make the fondue, place the chocolate, cream and malted milk powder in a small fondue pan (or saucepan) and heat very gently, stirring until melted. Divide the mixture between the raclette trays or individual gratin dishes. Diners can then add their marshmallows and pop them under the raclette grill (or a conventional grill/broiler) and cook until charred and gooey. Serve with the speculoos biscuits, sandwiching them together with the marshmallows if wished.

Note: The biscuit recipe makes plenty, so keep any extra in an airtight container for up to a week.

Bread and chocolate are an ever popular combination in Switzerland, and this sweet spin on the classic croûte fromage (melted cheese on bread) makes a great finale for any meal. Serve it with lashings of vanilla custard on the side.

Croûte chocolat

1 tablespoon butter, for greasing

400 g/14 oz. panettone, brioche or raisin bread (approx. 12 slices, about 10 cm/4 inches square and 1.5 cm/¾ inches thick)

2 bananas, sliced

250 g/9 oz. strawberries, hulled and halved

60 ml/4 tablespoons amaretto

150 g/5½ oz. dark/bittersweet chocolate, grated

vanilla custard, to serve

a 2-litre/quart baking dish, greased

Serves 6

Preheat the oven to 160°C fan/180°C/350°F/Gas 4.

Arrange the slices of panettone, brioche or raisin bread in overlapping rows in the prepared baking dish.

Insert the slices of banana and strawberry halves between the slices of panettone. Sprinkle with amaretto and then add a layer of grated chocolate on top.

Transfer to the preheated oven and bake for 25 minutes until puffed up and the chocolate has melted. Serve with plenty of vanilla custard.

An alternative take on the traditional pumpkin pie, this butternut squash and orange pie is great all year round, but is particularly satisfying during the colder months. Serve with a dollop of almond-flavoured sweetened cream.

Butternut squash & orange pie

1 x ready-made shortcrust pastry tart case/pie shell

FILLING

1 butternut squash (you need about 675 g/1½ lb. flesh), peeled and cut into 5-cm/2-in.chchunks

flavourless oil, for greasing

180 g /1 cup minus 1½ tablespoons dark brown soft sugar

3 eggs

170 g/200 ml evaporated milk

½ teaspoon ground ginger

1 teaspoon vanilla extract

finely grated zest of 1 orange

a pinch of salt

75 g/½ cup plus 1 tablespoon plain/all-purpose flour

2 tablespoons toasted flaked/slivered almonds

ALMOND CHANTILLY CREAM

300 ml/1¼ cups double/heavy cream

2 tablespoons icing/confectioners' sugar

a few drops of almond extract

a 25-cm/10-inch tart tin/pan

Serves 8

Preheat the oven to 160°C fan/180°C/350°F/Gas 4.

Place the squash on a lightly oiled baking sheet and bake for about 40 minutes, or until soft but not coloured. Once done, tip into a large mixing bowl and mash with a potato masher. Leave the oven on.

Use an electric hand whisk to beat the sugar and mashed squash together in a large bowl for a few minutes. Leave to cool slightly then add the eggs and whisk together until fully incorporated. Add the evaporated milk, ginger, vanilla extract, orange zest and a pinch of salt. Whisk until everything has completely combined. Finally fold in the flour, then whisk again until you have a very loose mixture.

Increase the oven temperature to 180°C fan/200°C/400°F/Gas 6.

Pour the mixture into the pastry case and scatter over the almonds. Bake for 40 minutes, it should be firm but have the slightest of wobbles when shaken. When done, remove from the oven and leave to cool in the tin.

Whisk the cream with the icing sugar and almond extract until you have soft peaks; don't over-whisk the cream. Taste, adding more almond extract if needed, then cover and chill in the fridge until ready to serve.

Slice the pie to serve, with dollops of the almond chantilly cream.

This indulgent dessert cake is moist and unctuous, fabulous eaten freshly baked and even better a day or two later. Walnuts and warming spices are complemented by a heady Greek brandy-infused syrup that soaks into the fluffy sponge.

Greek walnut cake

3 eggs

150 ml/²/₃ cup light olive oil or vegetable oil

150 ml/²/₃ cup whole milk

250 g/1¼ cups caster/granulated sugar

150 g/3 cups fresh brown breadcrumbs

150 g/1 cup semolina

200 g/2 scant cups coarse ground walnuts

1 tablespoon baking powder

1 tablespoon ground cinnamon

12 grates of nutmeg

¼ teaspoon ground cloves

walnut halves, to decorate

BRANDY SYRUP

200 g/1 cup caster/superfine sugar

3 strips of orange zest, plus extra finely grated zest to garnish

2 cinnamon sticks

½ teaspoon vanilla extract

60 ml/¼ cup brandy (preferably Greek)

a baking pan/high-sided baking sheet (about 30 x 20 cm/12 x 8 inches), lightly oiled

Serves 12

Preheat the oven to 180°C fan/200°C/400°F/Gas 6.

First make the syrup. Combine all the ingredients in a heavy-based saucepan and add 200 ml/¾ cup cold water. Set over a medium heat, bring to the boil, then immediately turn off the heat and leave in the pan to cool.

To make the cake batter, put the eggs, oil, milk and sugar in a large bowl and beat together using a hand-held electric whisk. In a separate bowl mix together the breadcrumbs, semolina, ground walnuts, baking powder and spices. Slowly fold the dry mixture into the wet mixture until fully combined – use a spatula to do this.

Pour the cake batter into the oiled baking pan and bake in the preheated oven for 30 minutes, or until a knife inserted into the centre comes out clean. Leave to cool in the pan for 15 minutes.

Run a knife through the cake in portion sizes, either in diamond shapes as pictured or squares. Spoon the room-temperature syrup slowly over the warm cake (you can discard the orange zest and cinnamon). You'll think you've made too much syrup but you haven't, keep going until all the syrup is used, then leave the cake to rest for minimum 1 hour (although it tastes even better the next day!). Once done, garnish with the walnut halves and a sprinkle of orange zest. It's sticky so serve it with forks.

This is a gentle sweet loaf that is great served for breakfast or brunch on a cold day. Infuse the dates with rooibos as its honeyed vanilla notes pair well with the pear and spelt for a moist loaf.

Pear, rooibos, date & spelt loaf

100 ml/scant ½ cup infused rooibos tea

150 g/5½ oz. dates, roughly chopped

1 teaspoon bicarbonate of soda/baking soda

180 g/1½ sticks butter, plus extra for greasing

100 g/½ cup raw cane/rapadura sugar

250 g/scant 2 cups wholemeal/whole-wheat spelt flour

1½ teaspoons baking powder

½ teaspoon ground cardamom (optional)

3 eggs, beaten

2 grated pears, plus 1 sliced on a mandoline to decorate

maple syrup, for brushing

a 900-g/2-lb. loaf pan

Makes 1 loaf

Preheat the oven to 140°C fan/160°C/325°F/Gas 3. Line the base and long sides
of the loaf pan with parchment paper, buttering the pan and paper.

In a bowl add the rooibos tea to the dates and the bicarbonate of soda/baking soda. Allow to sit and brew for 10 minutes.

Meanwhile, in a stand mixer mix the butter and sugar until light and fluffy. In a separate bowl mix the spelt flour, baking powder and cardamom, if using, and set aside. Gradually add the beaten eggs little by little into the butter and sugar, allowing it to mix in well. Turn off the machine and add the flour, the soaked and drained dates (discarding the soaking liquid) and the grated pears. Stir in by hand, making sure you do not over mix.

Pour the batter into the prepared loaf pan, top with the sliced reserved pear and bake in the preheated oven for around 45 minutes or until baked through and a skewer inserted into the centre comes out clean. Brush the top of the loaf and the pears with maple syrup and leave to cool in the pan for 15 minutes, then transfer to a wire rack to cool completely for a further 15 minutes before serving.

Seasonal drinks

Recreate this festive coffee shop drink in the comfort of your own home and indulge in this warming treat whenever you need a pick-me-up during the cold winter months.

Toffee nut latte

- 1–2 tablespoon toffee nut syrup, to taste
- 1–2 shots (30–60 ml/1–2 oz.) freshly brewed espresso coffee
- 250 ml/1 cup milk of your choice
- whipped cream (canned is fine)
- 1 teaspoon chopped nuts
- 1 teaspoon small toffee pieces or toffee sprinkles

milk steamer attachment or handheld electric milk frother

Serves 1

Pour the toffee nut syrup into a cup or heatproof glass and add the shots of hot coffee. Steam or froth the milk until hot and very foamy, then pour over the coffee and syrup mixture. Add a little whipped cream on top and sprinkle with chopped nuts and toffee pieces. Serve at once.

Perfect for any wintertime party, this thick, richly spiced latte is flavoured with sweetened pumpkin.

Pumpkin latte

- 375 ml/1½ cups milk of your choice
- 100 g/3½ oz. cooked sweet pumpkin, mashed, or canned pumpkin purée
- 3 tablespoons brown sugar (omit if using canned purée)
- ¼ teaspoon ground sweet cinnamon
- 250 ml/1 cup freshly brewed cafetière/French press or filter coffee
- whipped cream (canned is fine) and cinnamon sugar, to serve

balloon whisk

Serves 4

Put the milk, pumpkin, sugar (if using) and cinnamon in a saucepan and heat gently, whisking constantly until the mixture just reaches boiling point. Transfer to four cups or heatproof glasses and stir in the coffee.

Top with whipped cream and a dusting of cinnamon sugar. Serve at once.

In the run up to Christmas, why not blitz up this spiced cold brew coffee, which only takes a few minutes to prepare but after 24 hours steeping has delicious hints of festive spices with mellow coffee notes.

Coffee and chocolate make perfect partners, as this delicious drink proves. The addition of sweet, maple-flavoured cream makes this an indulgent treat and the perfect after-dinner drink.

Christmas morning cold brew

50 g/½ cup coffee beans

1 cinnamon stick

3 whole cloves

½ teaspoon vanilla bean powder

zest of 1 orange, removed using a zester to make long strands of peel

a little freshly grated nutmeg

TO SERVE

long cinnamon stick, to stir (optional)

dried orange slice

sugar, to taste (optional)

lidded 500-ml/2-cup container

muslin or coffee filter paper

fine-mesh sieve/strainer

Makes 400 ml/ 1¾ cups

Place the coffee beans, cinnamon stick, cloves, vanilla, orange zest and nutmeg in a blender and blitz for a few seconds so that the beans are coarsely ground. Do not grind to a fine powder otherwise this will make the coffee have an unpleasant texture. Place in a lidded container and pour over 400 ml/1¾ cups water and stir with a spoon. Put the lid on the container and place in the refrigerator for 24 hours to steep.

Remove from the refrigerator and strain through a muslin or use a coffee filter in a fine-mesh sieve. Make sure that all the coffee grounds are removed. The coffee is ready to serve once strained but can be stored in the refrigerator for up to 3 days (you can store for a few more days but the flavour will not be as good; it is best to make in small batches and use straight away).

To serve, pour into an ice-filled tumbler and garnish with a cinnamon stick and dried orange slice. Alternatively, serve warm if preferred.

Note: If you prefer a sweet coffee add a little sugar to taste and dissolve before serving.

Mocha maple coffee

500 ml/2 cups freshly brewed cafetière/French press or filter coffee

2 shots (60 ml/2 oz.) crème de cacao

125 ml/½ cup whipping cream

1 teaspoon maple syrup

roughly grated dark/ bittersweet chocolate, to sprinkle

balloon whisk

flat-bottomed barspoon or teaspoon

Serves 2

Pour the hot coffee into two heatproof glasses or cups and add a shot of crème de cacao to each one.

Lightly whisk the cream and maple syrup together until the mixture is foaming and thickened slightly. Slowly layer the cream over the surface of the coffee using a flat-bottomed barspoon or a teaspoon. Sprinkle with grated chocolate and serve at once.

Pecan pie is such a delicious dessert, and this pecan pie syrup gives a great taste and nutty texture to your coffee. The tiny pecan pieces act as an additional texture in the coffee, but if you prefer you can just omit the nuts and use the syrup for a smooth drink.

Pecan pie coffee

2–4 shots (60–120 ml/ 2–4 oz.) freshly brewed espresso coffee

600 ml/2½ cups milk of your choice

120 ml/½ cup double/ heavy cream

PECAN PIE SYRUP

1 tablespoon dark brown sugar

½ teaspoon ground sweet cinnamon

½ teaspoon vanilla bean paste or powder

1 tablespoon maple syrup

½ tablespoon golden or light corn syrup

10 g/2 teaspoons butter

20 g/scant ¼ cup pecan halves

milk steamer attachment or handheld electric milk frother

Serves 2

Make the pecan pie syrup first. In a saucepan heat the sugar, cinnamon, vanilla, both syrups, butter and 1 tablespoon water until the sugar has melted and you have a thick syrup. Reserve two whole pecan halves to decorate and finely chop the remainder. Stir the chopped pecans into the syrup. You need to use the syrup straight away as it will set as it cools.

Place a spoonful of the pecan pie syrup in the bottom of two heatproof glasses or cups and swirl the glasses so that the syrup coats the inside, then pour in the hot coffee. Steam or froth the milk until hot and foamy and pour into the glasses or cups. Whip the cream to soft peaks and place a spoonful on top of each drink. Top with the reserved pecan halves and drizzle over the remaining pecan pie syrup. Serve at once.

Eggnog is such a traditional Christmas tipple that it would be remiss not to include a frozen version. It's perfect to serve over the festive season as an adult 'boozy shake'. Make sure you use good-quality vanilla ice cream as this will really make a difference to the taste.

Eggnog shake

1 caramel cookie, such as Lotus Biscoff, crushed to fine crumbs with a rolling pin

½ tablespoon chocolate sundae sauce

60 ml/¼ cup Advocaat liqueur, plus extra to taste and to drizzle

3 scoops of vanilla ice cream

200 ml/¾ cup milk of your choice

1 tablespoon whipped double/heavy cream

paper drinking straws

Serves 1

Prepare a serving glass first. Place the cookie crumbs on a plate. Place the chocolate sauce on another plate and carefully roll the rim of the glass in the chocolate. Roll the chocolate dipped rim in the crumbs until the chocolate is coated. Save the leftover crumbs to sprinkle over the drink. Set the glass aside until you are ready to serve.

Place the Advocaat, ice cream and milk in a blender and blitz until all the ice cream is blended into the milk. Taste and if you want a boozier shake, add more Advocaat. Pour into the prepared glass taking care not to pour onto the decorated rim. Top the glass with the whipped cream and sprinkle over a few of the leftover cookie crumbs and a drizzle of Advocaat. Serve at once with drinking straws.

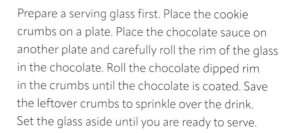

Licor 43 is a fruit and herb flavoured Spanish liqueur, which is used to perfection in this warming drink. The hot mulled cloudy apple recipe is delicious, so worth making a batch.

The toffee or caramel apple has been the adversary of teeth and dentists at many a carnival, fair or bonfire night; thankfully with this drink you're less likely to lose a tooth.

Hot spiced whiskey apple crumble

35 ml/1¼ oz. bourbon
or whiskey

15–20 ml/½–⅔ oz. Licor 43

150 ml/5 oz. Hot Mulled
Cloudy Apple
(see recipe below)

whipped cream and
toasted nuts, to garnish

Serves 1

Add the ingredients to a heatproof glass and gently stir. Garnish with whipped cream and toasted nuts and serve.

**HOT MULLED
CLOUDY APPLE**

2 cinnamon sticks

4 star anise

10 cloves

a pinch of salt

½ orange

1 litre/quart cloudy
apple juice

1 vanilla pod/bean, split
OR ¼ tsp vanilla extract

**Makes about
750 ml/3 cups**

Combine the ingredients together in a saucepan over medium heat. Simmer for 20 minutes. Use a ladle to serve and try to avoid putting any of the spices in the glass. Use as directed above, or enjoy as a mocktail.

Caramel apple toddy

60 ml/2 oz. Calvados

120 ml/4 oz. freshly brewed
hot English breakfast tea

10 ml/2 teaspoons caramel
syrup, plus extra to garnish

whipped cream, apple
slices and cinnamon
stick, to garnish

Serves 1

Add the ingredients to a heatproof glass and stir until the caramel syrup has dissolved. Garnish with whipped cream, apple slices, a cinnamon stick and extra syrup, and serve at once.

This is a rum-based version of a Negroni that marries the herbal complexity of the cocktail with the warm, intense and gently sweet character of rum. The drink works with a variety of rums, but the best results come from using a Jamaican pot-still rum such as Smith & Cross, which is packed full of complex spicy notes, and helps to make the perfect warming drink for the colder months.

Kingston negroni

25 ml/1 oz. Smith & Cross Jamaican Rum

25 ml/1 oz. red vermouth

25 ml/1 oz. Campari

a flamed orange zest, to garnish

Serves 1

Add the ingredients to an ice-filled mixing glass and stir. Strain into an ice-filled rocks glass. Finish and garnish with a flamed orange twist and serve at once.

Variation

For a less intense drink, mix 30 ml/1 oz. Cachaça (a Brazilian cane spirit) or white rum with 30 ml/1 oz. bianco vermouth, 15 ml/½ oz. Campari and 15 ml/½ oz. lime juice. Shake in an ice-filled cocktail shaker and pour (without straining) the entire contents of the shaker into a rocks glass. Add more ice and garnish with a lime wedge. Serve at once.

Fernet-Branca is an Italian amaro well known for its bittersweet qualities, but in this drink it is far more accessible as a part of a cosy, warming cocktail that will transport you to an Alpine ski lodge.

Hot buttered fernet

45 ml/1½ oz. Fernet-Branca

15 ml/½ oz. Bénédictine

15 ml/½ oz. bourbon

120 ml/4 oz. hot water

½ teaspoon good-quality butter (ideally salted)

cinnamon stick and orange zest, to garnish

Serves 1

Add the Fernet-Branca, Bénédictine and bourbon to a heatproof glass and top up with the hot water. Add the butter and stir until dissolved. Garnish with a cinnamon stick and an orange zest and serve at once.

If it's good enough for Champagne, it's good enough for Prosecco! Roll out the red carpet and serve this drink at any winter gathering for an added touch of glamour.

Prosecco classico

a few dashes of Angostura bitters

1 brown sugar cube

a dash of brandy

125 ml/4½ oz. well-chilled Prosecco

Serves 1

Drop several dashes of Angostura bitters onto the sugar cube and put it in a chilled Champagne flute. Add a dash of brandy, then add the Prosecco and serve at once.

A cocktail legend made even lovelier, thanks to a generous helping of Prosecco. The White Lady is a slinky, sophisticated 1920s classic and perfect to warm up a cold night.

Here a timeless classic is scaled down and served in a miniature cocktail glass to make the perfect aperitif for any festive party, add a stuffed olive to garnish and enjoy.

Prosecco white lady

35 ml/1½ oz. gin

15 ml/½ oz Cointreau

well-chilled Prosecco, to top up

15 ml/½ oz lemon juice

Serves 1

Pour the gin and Cointreau into a cocktail shaker half-filled with ice cubes. Stir until very cold, then strain into a chilled martini glass. Top up with Prosecco and the lemon juice and serve at once.

Mini martinis

15 ml/½ oz. Noilly Prat, or other dry vermouth

75 ml/3 oz. London dry gin (such as Beefeater)

2 stuffed green olives, to garnish (optional, see recipe intro)

Serves 2

Pour the vermouth and gin over cracked ice in a glass or metal mixing jug/pitcher. Stir to make the cocktail very cold. Strain into 2 small chilled cocktail glasses. Garnish with an olive, if using, and serve at once.

This variation on a Negroni is thought to have been invented by Erskine Gwynne, an American writer who lived in Paris and was a regular at Harry MacElhone's bar in that great city. The drink shared its name with the monthly magazine that Gwynne edited, 'The Boulevardier'.

Boulevardier

25 ml/1 oz. Maker's Mark Bourbon

25 ml/1 oz. Cocchi Vermouth di Torino, or other red vermouth

25 ml/1 oz. Campari

an orange zest, to garnish

Serves 1

Add all the ingredients to an ice-filled mixing glass and stir vigorously. Strain into a coupe glass, garnish with a piece of orange peel and serve at once.

A lighter and less sweet version of The Boulevardier (see above).

Old pal

25 ml/1 oz. rye whiskey

25 ml/1 oz. Cocchi Americano

25 ml/1 oz. Campari

a lemon zest, to garnish

Serves 1

Add the ingredients to an ice-filled mixing glass and stir vigorously. Strain into a rocks glass (with ice if liked), garnish with a lemon spiral and serve at once.

A red wine float provides a delectably festive twist on the classic whiskey sour.

New York sour

50 ml/1²/₃ oz. Bulleit Bourbon

25 ml/³/₄ oz. fresh lemon juice

25 ml/³/₄ oz. sugar syrup

1 dash of Angostura bitters

20 ml/²/₃ oz. egg white

25 ml/³/₄ oz. red wine

an edible flower, to garnish

Serves 1

Combine all the drink ingredients, except the wine, in a cocktail shaker and 'dry' shake without ice to emulsify the egg white. Add a scoop of cubed ice, then shake hard and strain into a small wine glass over cubed ice. Pour the red wine slowly over the back of a bar spoon or teaspoon to 'float' a layer of red wine over the cocktail. Garnish with an edible flower and serve at once.

Named after a voting district in Boston once famous for its political corruption, the ward eight is a somewhat forgotten classic cocktail that pairs rye whiskey with orange juice.

Ward eight

50 ml/1²/₃ oz. Michter's Straight Rye Whiskey

25 ml/³/₄ oz. fresh lemon juice

25 ml/³/₄ oz. fresh orange juice

7.5 ml/1½ teaspoons grenadine

10 ml/2 teaspoons sugar syrup (or to taste)

an orange wedge and Luxardo maraschino cherry, to garnish

Serves 1

Add all the drink ingredients to a cocktail shaker with a scoop of cubed ice and shake hard. Strain into a chilled coupe glass, garnish with an orange wedge and a cherry and serve at once.

Index

Recipe Credits

JULIA CHARLES
Mini martinis

JESSE ESTES
New York Sour
Ward Eight

LAURA GLADWIN
Prosecco Classico
Prosecco White Lady

KATHY KORDALIS
Pecorino Arancini with
  Roasted Cherry Tomato
  Sauce
Pear, Rooibos, Date & Spelt
  Loaf
Poached Trout, Shaved
  Carrot, Corn & Amaranth
  with a Mustard & Dill
  Dressing
Rice Pancakes with Spiced
  Potatoes

THEO A. MICHAELS
Butternut Squash & Orange
  Pie
Greek Walnut Cake
Harvest Pie
Meatless Moussaka
Oven-baked Broccoli & Blue
  Cheese Gnocchi
Oxtail Stew with Dumplings
Poached Pears with Orange
  Blossom Chantilly Cream
Red Lentil Tarka Dhal with
  Honey Roasted
  Cauliflower
Rich Mushroom Ragu on
  Polenta
Roasted Radicchio with Blue
  Cheese Dressing
Roast Squash & Lentil Salad
Salmon 'Nduja Wellington
Smoked Haddock on
  Sourdough
Smoky Black Bean Stew with
  Sweet Potatoes & Minted
  Yogurt Dressing

HANNAH MILES
Brown Butter Baked Potato
  Soup
Christmas Morning Cold
  Brew
Creamy Cauliflower & Blue
  Cheese Soup
Curried Parsnip Soup
Eggnog Shake
Mocha Maple Coffee
Pearl Barley Broth
Pecan Pie Coffee
Pumpkin Latte
Roasted Cauliflower Soup
  with Toasted Almonds &
  Pickled Florets
Roasted Garlic Soup
Roasted Pumpkin Soup
Sausage & Cabbage Soup
Three Bean Soup
Toffee Nut Latte

LOUISE PICKFORD
Bagna Cauda
Baked French Onion Soup
Baked Orchard Fruit
  Cobbler with Cinnamon
  Crème Fraîche
Baked Pumpkin & Spelt
  Risotto
Baked Savoury Bread &
  Four-cheese Pudding with
  Beetroot Jam
Boston Baked Beans
Cheddar & CalvadosFondue
  with Apple Rosti
Chicken & Duck Fondue
  with Tunisian Relish
Classic Raclette
Comté with Caramelized
  Chestnuts, Raisins &
  Hazelnuts
Coq au Vin
Creamy Smoked Fish Pies
  with Scallop Potatoes
Creamy Turkey &
  Mushroom Puff Pastry Pie
Croûte Chocolat
Dolcelatte & Sweet Potato
  Salad with Caramelized
  Pecans
Doughnuts with Salted
  Bourbon Caramel
Duck & Sausage Cassoulet
Frozen Summer Berries with
  White Chocolate Custard
Ginger & Crab Fondue
Goat's Cheese Bruschetta
  with Roasted Beetroot
Goat's Cheese Rounds with
  Honey, Thyme & Grapes
Halloumi & Fattoush Salad
  with Crispy Flatbreads
Hot Salmon Kedgeree with
  Coriander & Lime
Hungarian Goulash with
  Cornbread Dumplings
Individual Smoked Fish
  Fondues
Lamb Fondue with Toasted
  Baharat
Malted Milk S'mores
Moroccan Lamb with Dates
  & Olives
Neuchâtel Fondue
Orange & Cardamom
  Fondue
Oven-baked Meatballs with
  Cheesy Tomato Sauce
Pasta e Fagioli
Peaches with Raclette &
  Cinnamon
Pizza Ring with Melted
  Camembert
Ploughman's Fondue
Polenta Fries with
  Mayonnaise &
  Chimichurri
Porcini Fonduta
Pumpkin, Fig & Maple Syrup
  Steamed Pudding
Roasted Pork Belly in Cider
  with Crispy Crackling
Roasted Pumpkin Fondue
  with Crispy Sage
Roasted Turkey Breast with
  Prosciutto & Cranberry
  Gravy
Slow-braised Duck with
  Spices, Soy Sauce & Pears
Slow-roasted Pork Ribs with
  Cabbage & Apple Slaw
Sri Lankan Fish Curry
Swiss Fondue Fritters
Tartiflette
Twice-baked Cheese
  Soufflés with Beaufort
  Cream
Upside-down Pineapple &
  Coconut Cake with Rum
  Cream
Vietnamese-style Miso, Red
  Wine & Caramel Beef
  Cheeks
Welsh Rabbit with Mustard
  Onions
White Bean and Rosemary
  Soup with Bacon
  Pangrattato

SHELAGH RYAN
Butternut Squash with Eggs,
  Cavolo Nero, Feta &
  Jalapeño Zhoug

DAVID T. SMITH
Boulevardier
Caramel Apple Toddy
Hot Buttered Fernet
Hot Spiced Whiskey Apple
  Crumble
Kingston Negroni
Old Pal

Photography Credits

ED ANDERSON
Page 15.

PETER CASSIDY
Pages 183 and 187.

MOWIE KAY
Pages 33, 71, 92, 108, 111, 112,
  123, 124, 128, 132, 136, 139,
  147, 153, 170, 173, 174 and 181.

ALEX LUCK
Pages 14, 17, 18, 21, 22, 25, 26,
  29, 30, 178, 179, 182, 184,
  185, 186 and 189.

NASSIMA ROTHACKER
Page 4.

IAN WALLACE
Pages 1, 2, 5, 7, 10, 11, 13, 34,
  36, 37, 38, 40, 41, 42, 43, 45,
  48, 49, 51, 52, 53, 54, 55,
  56, 59, 60, 63, 64, 65, 66,
  67, 68, 69, 76, 79, 80, 81, 84,
  87, 88, 90, 91, 95, 96, 99,
  100, 102, 103, 104, 106, 107,
  114, 115, 116, 118, 119, 120,
  126, 127, 131, 140, 143, 144,
  150, 151, 154, 156, 157, 158,
  161, 162, 163, 165, 166, 168
  and 169.

KATE WHITTAKER
Pages 72, 75 and 85.

CLARE WINFIELD
Pages 117, 146 and 168.